# dish

## Contents

| | |
|---|---|
| **INTRODUCTION** | 4 |
| **COME FOR A DRINK** | 8 |
| **STAY FOR DINNER** | 36 |
| **FIRE UP THE BARBIE** | 66 |
| **BRING A SALAD** | 100 |
| **BURGER MANIA** | 136 |
| **WHAT'S FOR DESSERT?** | 152 |
| **FILL THE TINS** | 182 |
| **SAUCY BITS** | 208 |
| **MEASUREMENTS + CONVERSIONS** | 220 |
| **INDEX** | 224 |
| **ACKNOWLEDGEMENTS** | 239 |

# *dish* summer

Long days, warm nights – summer was made for easy entertaining.

Sarah Tuck and Claire Aldous

Photography by Josh Griggs and Sarah Tuck

# Sarah Tuck

I am thrilled to introduce you to our second-ever *dish* cookbook – *dish SUMMER*.

For those of you who are already regular *dish* magazine readers, you'll know that we put a good deal of focus on creating recipes that are in tune with the seasons, wherever possible using fresh, local produce. Each season has its own appeal. Autumn, with its nip in the air, is a time for harvest meals, while winter invites us to hunker down with slow-cooks and indulgent puds, and in wet and wild spring, we take baby steps toward making lighter fare.

But summer? Summer is a time of lazy days at the beach, drinks on the deck and late dinners al fresco in the last of the setting sun. Produce is abundant – asparagus, berries, stone fruit, avocados and sweetcorn are all at their best – and seafood makes its way onto the menu more than at any other time of year. Summer is a time for casual entertaining, for weekends (or weeks) away, for boating, picnics and impromptu barbecues. I think it would be fair to say that in this book, *dish* has you covered.

The sections are divided into classic New Zealand sections. In "Come for Drink", we share some of our favourite nibbly bits to enjoy with a cold beer on a hot day. From the stunning Oysters on the Half Shell with mignonette or Japanese-style dressings (page 16), to the moreish Salt and Pepper Squid (page 22), there are bites for everything from watching the cricket to pool-side cocktail hour. For the drinks, we range from a full-grunt Negroni (page 34) to a Bloody-Mary-meets-chilled-beer Michelada (page 26).

Who hasn't invited visitors to "Stay for Dinner"? Here, pizzas get the easy gourmet treatment, cheeky pastas are studded with sun-ripened tomatoes and fish meets batter with spectacular results in our Best-ever Fresh Catch Beer-battered Fish (page 60). Next stop, it's barbecue country, with everything from Grilled Zucchini with Tzatziki and Kasundi (page 70) to Beer Can Chicken with White Barbecue Sauce (page 88). Next time you're asked to "Bring a Salad", you won't have to think twice, with a fabulous line-up to choose from – one of my favourites is the Seeded Slaw (page 104). We reckon there's no better time of year to squash the top down on a loaded burger and from page 136 we present six stonking great options to have on rotation. The Chorizo and Garlic Prawn Burger (page 144)? Sensational!

Dinner is done and there's just a wee bit of room left for a sweet treat to round out the meal – so "What's for Dessert?". How about a sexy little Chilled Espresso Martini Affogato (page 156) or a gorgeous Rhubarb and Strawberry Frangipane Tart (page 168)? When it comes to days at the beach or picnics in the park, there's nothing like having a little something to take along. The One-pot Chocolate Cake with Sour Cream and Chocolate Frosting (page 194) goes down a treat with a morning coffee, while the Sticky Fingers Ginger Loaf with Butterscotch Glaze (page 190) is the perfect partner for a thermos of tea in the afternoon.

As you can see, I could wax lyrical about summer and the recipes in this book until the cows come home. But now it's time for me to stop, and for you to start getting stuck in. I hope *dish SUMMER* will be your go-to warm weather cookbook for many years to come!

# Claire Aldous

When I think of summer food, my heart does a little dance with the anticipation of the long, warm, sunny days and evenings ahead.

I can put away the heavy casserole dishes, the soup ladles and stocks of winter cooking and ready myself for ingredients that are light and fresh. Asparagus, avocados, juicy ripe tomatoes and fragrant basil and mint are lining up waiting to be transformed into delicious dishes that are bursting with sunshine.

With the book divided into simple-to-follow chapters, there are recipes for everything from quick midweek meals – I'm thinking of you, Fresh Fennel, Salami and Chilli Pizza (page 48) – to crowd-pleasers for the barbecue, like the get-ahead Beef Short Ribs (page 90). Standing at the kitchen bench prepping cobs of corn for the Grilled Corn with Whipped Ricotta and Smoky Chilli Butter (page 78) or slicing stone fruit then sparking up the barbecue to cook the Boozy Barbecued Stone Fruit Parcels (page 164) outside, is there anything more joyful?!

There's a sociable aspect to summer cooking as well that gives me energy and a sense of connection. Because most summer recipes tend towards being quick to cook, there's plenty of scope for impromptu gatherings. I'll often invite friends over for a casual lunch or dinner and the cooking is so easy – the Luscious Tomatoes, Baked Eggplant and Mozzarella Salad (page 120) is perfect alongside our simple Barbecued Butterflied Leg of Lamb (page 96).

And to finish off the meal, it's pure joy to welcome in plump, locally grown strawberries that instantly bring back memories of picking strawberries 'out west' with my darling mum as a child, then using them to make one of my all-time favourite desserts, Sarah's Rhubarb and Strawberry Frangipane Tarts (page 168).

I have a few rules for cooking in summer and you might find them helpful in your own kitchen: I always make double of a dressing, flavoured butter or marinade and keep them on hand, as they're so useful for when I find myself saying, "Come for dinner!" when really I have no idea what I'll cook!

I also shop more frequently to take advantage of the ripening cycles of summer fruit and vegetables and I'll look out for farmers' markets and local stalls that pop up selling corn and watermelon and fruit from backyards.

*dish SUMMER* is packed with our well-loved and much-cooked recipes that I hope will find a place in your kitchen and allow you to focus on enjoying the love and laughter of being in the company of good friends.

Summer cooking – it's worth waiting the whole year for, and it's worth sharing!

# COME FOR A DRINK

*Whether gathering friends for a late-afternoon beer after a day at the beach or breaking out the cocktail shaker for something a little fancy, there's no better time of year to put the call out to 'come for a drink'! It's the thought of what nibbles to serve that can often have hosts scratching their heads in consternation. We make it easy with a round-up of simple, tasty morsels to share – from Chicken Katsu Sliders (page 14) to Prawn, Zucchini and Lemongrass Fritters (page 18), there's something to suit all-comers. Let's turn the music a up a bit, find a spot in the shade and raise a glass to summer drinks.*

# Whipped Avocado with Silken Tofu, Lime and Jalapeño (gf) (v)

*Silken tofu and ripe avocado give this dip a lusciously thick, creamy texture, with the jalapeños and lime adding a refreshing bite. Serve with crudités and small grissini bread sticks.*

**MAKES ABOUT 2 CUPS**

300 grams silken tofu, drained

1 large ripe avocado

½ packed cup coriander, roughly chopped

3 tablespoons olive oil

¼ cup sliced jalapeños in brine, drained

1 tablespoon jalapeño brine

finely grated zest 2 limes

2 tablespoons lime juice

2 cloves garlic, crushed

1 teaspoon caster sugar

1½ teaspoons sea salt

**TO SERVE**
toasted sesame seeds

olive oil

Place all the ingredients in a food processor and blend until silky smooth, or place in a deep bowl and use a stick blender.

**TO SERVE:** Transfer to a serving bowl and top with sesame seeds and a drizzle of olive oil.

# Prawn and Chorizo Kebabs with Smoked Paprika Mayo (gf)

*These smoky, juicy little morsels are incredibly moreish and fantastic served alongside a cold beer.*

**MAKES 16 SKEWERS**

**KEBABS**

2 tablespoons tomato paste

1 teaspoon smoked paprika

2 cloves garlic, crushed

½ teaspoon cumin seeds

finely grated zest 1 lemon

1 tablespoon lemon juice

2 tablespoons olive oil

sea salt and ground pepper

16 large raw prawns, peeled, with tail on

2 x cured gluten-free chorizo sausages, about 250 grams total, each sliced into 8 rounds

**SMOKED PAPRIKA MAYO**

½ cup good-quality egg mayonnaise

1 roasted red capsicum, peeled, seeded and roughly chopped

2 cloves garlic, crushed

1 teaspoon smoked paprika

**EQUIPMENT:** 16 thin metal or wooden skewers.

**KEBABS:** Thoroughly combine all the ingredients in a large bowl. Place a piece of chorizo in the curve of each prawn and push a skewer through, passing through both ends of the prawn and the chorizo. Cover and refrigerate until ready to cook.

**SMOKED PAPRIKA MAYO:** Blitz all the ingredients in a food processor and season.

**TO COOK:** Heat a frying pan over a medium heat and lightly oil. Cook the skewers until the prawns are golden and cooked, about 2 minutes per side. Serve with the mayo.

# Chicken Katsu Sliders

*These mini crispy chicken burgers always disappear fast and are so easy to put together. Look for small dinner rolls at good bakeries.*

**MAKES 10 SLIDERS**

3 boneless, skinless chicken thighs

½ cup plain flour

2 teaspoons curry powder

sea salt and ground pepper

2 large eggs, lightly beaten

1 tablespoon soy sauce

1½ cups panko crumbs

vegetable oil, for cooking

knob of butter

**TO ASSEMBLE**

10 slider buns or small dinner rolls, halved and toasted

good-quality egg mayonnaise

American mustard

purchased coleslaw

sliced pickles

Cut the chicken into pieces roughly the same size as the buns.

Place the flour and curry powder in a bowl and season with salt and pepper. Whisk the eggs and soy together in another bowl and place the panko crumbs in a third bowl.

Dust the chicken in the flour mixture, shaking off the excess. Dip in the egg mixture, then coat in the crumbs, pressing them on well to adhere.

Heat a little oil in a large frying pan over a medium heat, then add the butter. When sizzling, cook the chicken until golden and fully cooked through. Drain on kitchen towels.

**TO ASSEMBLE:** Spread both halves of the buns with some mayonnaise and a swirl of mustard. Top the bottoms with slaw, chicken and pickles. Sandwich with the tops and serve immediately.

# Oysters on the Half Shell

*It goes without saying that whatever type of oyster you choose, they must be absolutely fresh on the day of serving. Each of the dressings is enough for a dozen oysters.*

**MAKES 24 OYSTERS**

24 oysters on the half shell

**MIGNONETTE DRESSING**
⅓ cup champagne vinegar or chardonnay vinegar

1 teaspoon caster sugar

3 tablespoons finely chopped shallots

sea salt

**JAPANESE-STYLE DRESSING**
2 tablespoons soy sauce

2 tablespoons rice wine vinegar

2 teaspoons sesame oil

3 tablespoons thinly sliced pickled ginger

**MIGNONETTE DRESSING:** Whisk the ingredients together and spoon over 12 of the oysters on the half shell. Season with a sprinkle of sea salt.

**JAPANESE-STYLE DRESSING:** Whisk the soy, vinegar and sesame oil together, then stir in the ginger. Spoon over 12 of the oysters on the half shell.

# Prawn, Zucchini and Lemongrass Fritters (gf)

*A good fritter is always a popular finger food option at summer parties. We topped ours with a dab of crème fraîche, crispy shallots and coriander. Other options include sour cream and chilli jam; mayo mixed with a little wasabi paste and coriander; or thick coconut yoghurt, toasted shredded coconut and sliced fresh chilli.*

**MAKES ABOUT 20**

½ cup ground almonds (almond meal)

1 tablespoon chia seeds

2 cloves garlic, crushed

1 tablespoon grated fresh ginger

1 large egg

¼ cup thick coconut cream

sea salt and ground pepper

1 medium zucchini

½ cup corn kernels, thawed if frozen, finely chopped

200 grams raw peeled prawns, finely chopped

1 long red chilli, seeded and finely chopped

1 large stalk lemongrass, grated on a fine microplane grater

good handful coriander, finely chopped

rice bran oil, for cooking

Combine the almonds, chia seeds, garlic, ginger, egg and coconut cream in a large bowl and season well. Set aside for 10 minutes to thicken.

Grate the zucchini on the large side of a box grater, then measure out ½ well-packed cup. Scatter over a clean tea towel, roll up tightly and squeeze out all the moisture.

Add the squeezed zucchini, corn, prawns, chilli, lemongrass and coriander to the almond batter and stir together. Season.

Heat a little oil in a frying pan over a medium heat and add spoonfuls of the mixture, gently flattening each one a little for even cooking.

Cook for about 2 minutes each side, turning carefully until golden and fully cooked through.

Transfer to kitchen towels and keep warm in a low oven while making the remaining fritters.

**TO SERVE:** Place on a platter and top with your chosen garnish (see recipe introduction for ideas).

dish.co.nz | DISH 19

# Prawns with Nectarines, Mozzarella and Prosciutto (gf)

*This is such a simple starter salad, you need to ensure the fruit is pristine and use a really good, fruity extra-virgin olive oil.*

**SERVES 6**

**PRAWNS**

¼ cup olive oil

¼ cup basil leaves

2 cloves garlic, crushed

zest 1 lemon

18 large raw prawns, peeled with tails attached

sea salt and ground pepper

**TO ASSEMBLE**

4 ripe nectarines or peaches

1 lemon

12 slices of prosciutto

2 x 125-gram balls fresh buffalo mozzarella in whey

extra-virgin olive oil, for drizzling

fresh basil leaves

**PRAWNS:** Process the oil, basil, garlic and lemon zest in a food processor until smooth. Pour over the prawns, season and toss together. Heat a large frying pan over a medium-high heat and fry the prawns until just cooked through.

**TO ASSEMBLE:** Cut the nectarines or peaches into wedges. Arrange on serving plates and squeeze over a little lemon juice. Drape the prosciutto over the nectarines. Rip the mozzarella into pieces and tuck into the salad along with the prawns. Drizzle over a little extra-virgin olive oil, sprinkle over a few basil leaves, season and serve.

# Salt and Pepper Squid

*A bowl of tender squid makes a delicious bite to enjoy with a drink. Serve as is or wrap in lettuce with cucumber slices and bean sprouts.*

**SERVES 4 WITH A DRINK**

300 grams squid tubes, thawed

¼ cup plain flour

¼ cup cornflour

2 teaspoons sea salt

1 teaspoon ground pepper

½ teaspoon chilli powder, or more to taste

vegetable oil for frying

**TO SERVE**

½ cup good-quality egg mayonnaise

2-3 teaspoons wasabi paste

small handful coriander, chopped

1 long red chilli, finely chopped

2 limes, cut into wedges

Cut the squid tubes into ½ cm-thick rings.

Put the flour, cornflour, salt, pepper and chilli powder in a large bowl and crush together with the back of a teaspoon to combine. Add the squid, tossing to coat well.

Heat 2cm of oil in a frying pan until it begins to shimmer.

Add the squid in batches, shaking off excess flour, and cook for about 2 minutes, until lightly golden and tender. Remove with a slotted spoon and place on kitchen towels to drain. Keep warm in a low oven until all the squid are cooked.

**TO SERVE:** Combine the mayonnaise and wasabi paste. Serve the squid topped with the combined coriander and chilli, alongside the lime wedges and mayonnaise.

# Mexican Fish Tacos with Avocado and Jalapeño Sauce

*Tacos are always a hit at my house and this delicious avocado sauce pulls everything together. Sometimes I make it to serve with taco chips as a fabulous dip.*

**SERVES 4-5**

1 large avocado

⅓ cup packed coriander leaves, roughly chopped, plus extra to serve

¼ cup sliced jalapeños in brine, drained

1 tablespoon jalapeño brine

2 tablespoons lime or lemon juice

2 cloves garlic, crushed

sea salt

700 grams fish fillets

¼ cup purchased Mexican spice mix (I used Culley's)

olive oil for cooking

**TO SERVE**

10 x 15cm flour tortillas, warmed

250 grams sour cream

1 bag purchased coleslaw

lime wedges

Put the avocado flesh, coriander, jalapeños, brine, lime or lemon juice, garlic and a good pinch of salt in a food processor. Process until smooth, scraping down the sides if needed. Transfer to a bowl.

Cut the fish into large bite-sized pieces and toss with the spice mix.

Heat a little oil in a large frying pan and cook the fish until golden and just cooked through. *You may have to do this in batches.*

**TO SERVE:** Spread the warm tortillas with sour cream, then top with the coleslaw and the fish. Dollop over the avocado sauce and extra coriander. Squeeze over the lime wedges, then roll up and eat immediately.

# Michelada

*Bloody Mary meets a chilled beer – who knew this combo would work so well? I love mine heavily spiced with hot sauce.*

**SERVES 1**

ice cubes

tomato juice

tequila

Worcestershire sauce

hot sauce

beer

lime wedges

Coat the rim of a tall glass in Chilli and Celery Salt (see recipe below). Fill the glass with ice cubes. One-third fill the glass with tomato juice, then add 1 tablespoon tequila, 2 splashes Worcestershire sauce and 2-3 splashes hot sauce, or more to taste (we used a chipotle hot sauce). Top up with chilled beer (we used a Mexican beer, Sol), squeeze over a lime wedge, give it a stir and serve.

## Chilli and Celery Salt Coating

**MAKES ENOUGH FOR 4 GLASSES**

1 tablespoon ground chilli

1 tablespoon sea salt, roughly crushed

1 teaspoon celery salt

1 egg white, lightly beaten until frothy

Combine the chilli and both salts in a saucer. Dip the rim of a glass in egg white, then in the salt mix. Makes enough salt for several glasses. Store in an airtight jar.

# Mushroom Arancini (v)

*I have been making arancini for approximately a billion years – because they always hit the spot and are easier to make than you think!*

**MAKES 33**

10 grams dried porcini mushrooms

1 cup boiling water

¼ cup olive oil

1 red onion, finely chopped

5 cloves garlic, crushed

½ teaspoon chilli flakes

sea salt and black pepper

1 cup arborio rice

¼ cup white wine

3¼ cups good-quality vegetable or chicken stock

50 grams butter

250 grams portobello mushrooms, quite finely chopped

2 sprigs fresh thyme

⅔ cup freshly grated parmesan

125-gram block mozzarella, cut into 1.5cm cubes

4 cups breadcrumbs

3 large eggs, whisked

5 cups high-heat cooking oil

good-quality garlic or truffle aioli, to serve

Cover the porcini mushrooms with the boiling water and set aside.

Heat half the olive oil in a big saucepan and add the onion, garlic, chilli flakes, salt and pepper. Cook for 10 minutes over a medium-low heat, then add the rice and cook, stirring, for a further 2 minutes. Add the wine and cook for 2 minutes while heating the stock in a separate saucepan.

Drain the dried porcini mushrooms, reserving the liquid. Finely chop the porcini mushrooms and add to the risotto. Begin adding the hot stock a ladle at a time, stirring and allowing the liquid to be absorbed before adding the next quantity. Meanwhile, heat the remaining oil with the butter in a large frying pan. Add the portobello mushrooms and thyme, season well with salt and pepper and cook, stirring, over a high heat for 7-8 minutes.

When you have added all the stock and the risotto is tender to the bite and has a creamy consistency (after about 20 minutes), remove it from the heat and stir through the grated parmesan and cooked portobello mushrooms. Transfer to a container and chill until cool.

Take tablespoonfuls of cold risotto and poke a mozzarella cube in the middle. Roll into a ball, then roll into breadcrumbs to coat. Repeat for all the risotto, then, starting with the first ball again, dip each ball into the whisked egg and roll in the breadcrumbs again. You should end up with about 33. Store in the fridge for at least an hour before cooking and up to overnight.

Heat the cooking oil in a large, deep saucepan until it has a sheen on the surface and a piece of bread dropped in turns golden in 20 seconds. Fry the arancini in batches of 5-6 at a time for 3-4 minutes, until golden and heated through. Serve immediately with aioli.

# Reuben Sliders

*These are spectacular served as the evening progresses and appetites are growing.*

**MAKES 12**

**RUSSIAN DRESSING**
1⅓ cups good-quality egg mayonnaise

⅓ cup tomato sauce

3 teaspoons horseradish

1 teaspoon ground paprika

sea salt and ground pepper

**TO ASSEMBLE**
12 mini brioche rolls

150 grams grated gruyère

250 grams pastrami

2 cups sauerkraut

12 cocktail gherkins

**EQUIPMENT:** 12 small skewers.

**RUSSIAN DRESSING:** Whisk all of the ingredients together and store in a sealed container in the fridge for up to a week.

**TO ASSEMBLE:** Preheat the oven to 180°C regular bake.

Split the slider buns in half. Top the bases with the grated gruyère and heat in the oven with the slider tops until the cheese has melted. Top the bases with pastrami, Russian Dressing and sauerkraut. Secure the slider lids in place with a gherkin-spiked skewer and serve immediately.

# Horse's Neck

*Giddy up...*

**SERVES 1**

1 lemon

ice

3 dashes Angostura bitters

60ml bourbon

ginger ale, to top up

Peel the zest from the lemon in one continuous spiral and trim the edges neatly. Coil it around a chopstick to encourage it to twirl, then place in a glass with plenty of ice. The ice will help to secure the lemon spiral in place around the edge of the glass. Add the bitters and bourbon and top with ginger ale to serve.

# Morning Start-up

*Ladies and gentlemen – start your engines!*

**SERVES 1**

60ml stout or dark beer

30ml coffee liqueur

champagne, to top up

Combine the stout and liqueur in a champagne flute, then slowly add the champagne by pouring it carefully over the back of a teaspoon. Serve immediately.

# Christmas Champagne Cocktail

*We won't tell if you keep the good times going with this one well into the new year...*

**SERVES 1**

1 lemon

30ml gin

15ml freshly squeezed lemon juice

15ml elderflower liqueur

2 dashes orange bitters

champagne, to top up

Peel a strip of lemon and trim it to be quite skinny. Put the gin, lemon juice and liqueur in a champagne flute. Add the bitters and top with champagne. Serve garnished with the lemon peel.

# Negroni

*One of our all-time favourite drinks, the Italian negroni is not for the faint-hearted. Bitter and delicious, it is summer in a glass!*

**SERVES 1**

30ml gin

30ml Campari

30ml vermouth rosso

strip of orange peel

Put the gin, Campari and vermouth together in a cocktail shaker with plenty of ice. Stir well, then strain into a glass over (ideally) a large cube or ball of ice. Squeeze the orange peel over the glass to release some of the oils, then twist and add as a garnish.

# Gibson Martini

*The Gibson martini, traditionally made with gin (although you can substitute vodka), uses a pickled cocktail onion in place of the usual olive to add an umami undertone to the classic cocktail.*

**SERVES 1**

70ml gin

15ml dry vermouth

1-2 cocktail onions, drained

Chill a martini glass in the fridge. Put the gin and vermouth into a cocktail shaker with plenty of ice and stir. Strain into the chilled cocktail glass and garnish with 1-2 cocktail onions.

# Elderflower G&T

*Pretty and delicate, the elderflower gin and tonic is the perfect drink for a festive, sunny afternoon gathering.*

**SERVES 1**

50ml gin

10ml elderflower syrup

tonic water to taste

1 slice lemon

edible flowers, garnish

Pour the gin and elderflower syrup into a glass and add plenty of ice and tonic to taste. Garnish with the lemon slice and edible flowers.

# STAY FOR DINNER

*It's an invitation proffered around New Zealand on a regular basis, and even more so in the summer months. Not wanting to let the fun times end after an afternoon get-together, we have a quick rummage in the fridge, then nip to the supermarket to grab a few extras so we can throw together an impromptu feast. Nothing could be easier than Spicy Salami, Prosciutto and Mozzarella Pizza (page 44) or Baked Prawns with Lemon and Feta (page 56). Baked Spanish Rice with Chicken and Chorizo (page 62) is perfect to feed a crowd while Claire's Best-ever Fresh Catch Beer-battered Fish and Chips (page 60) is almost life-changing.*

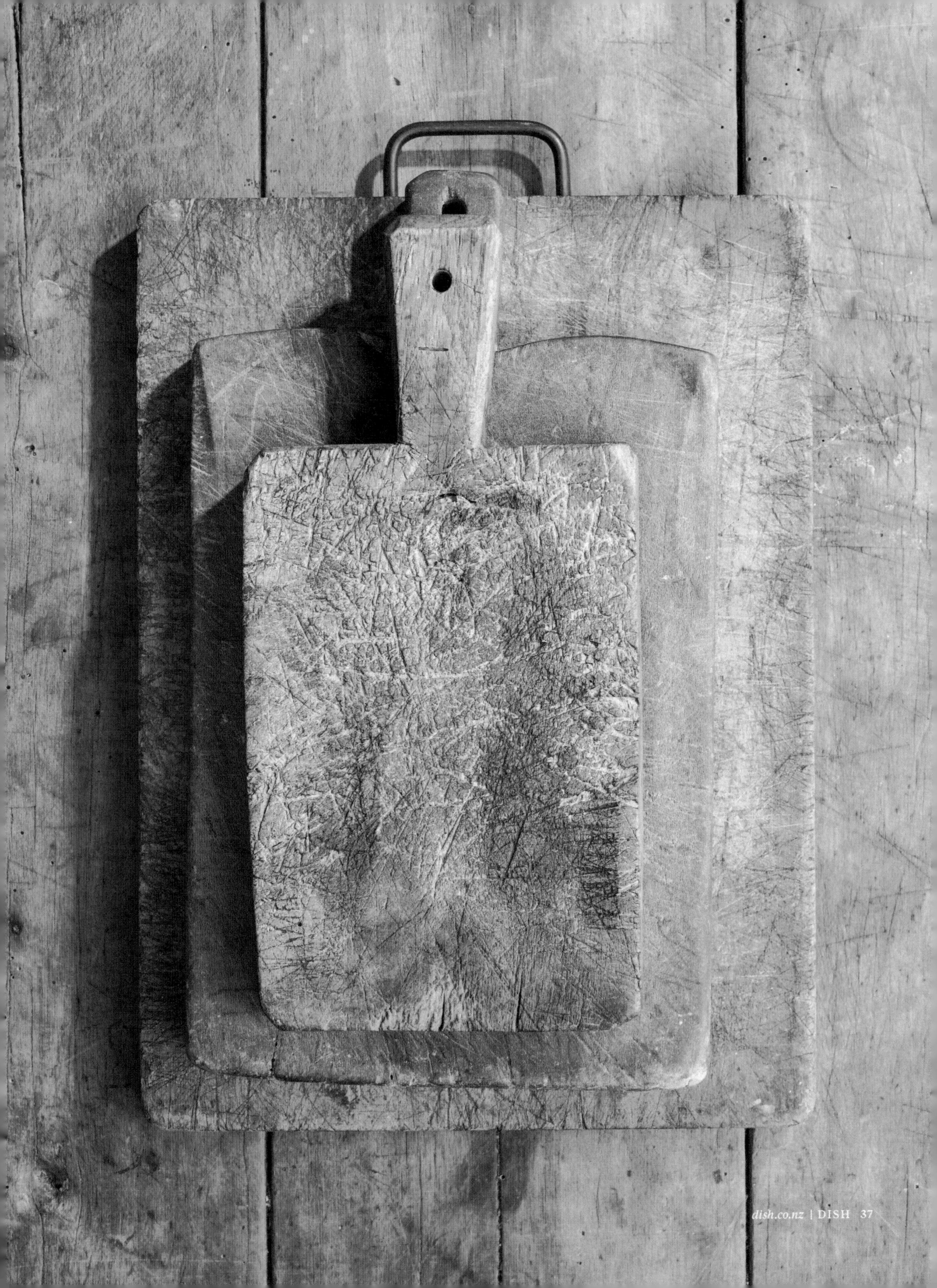

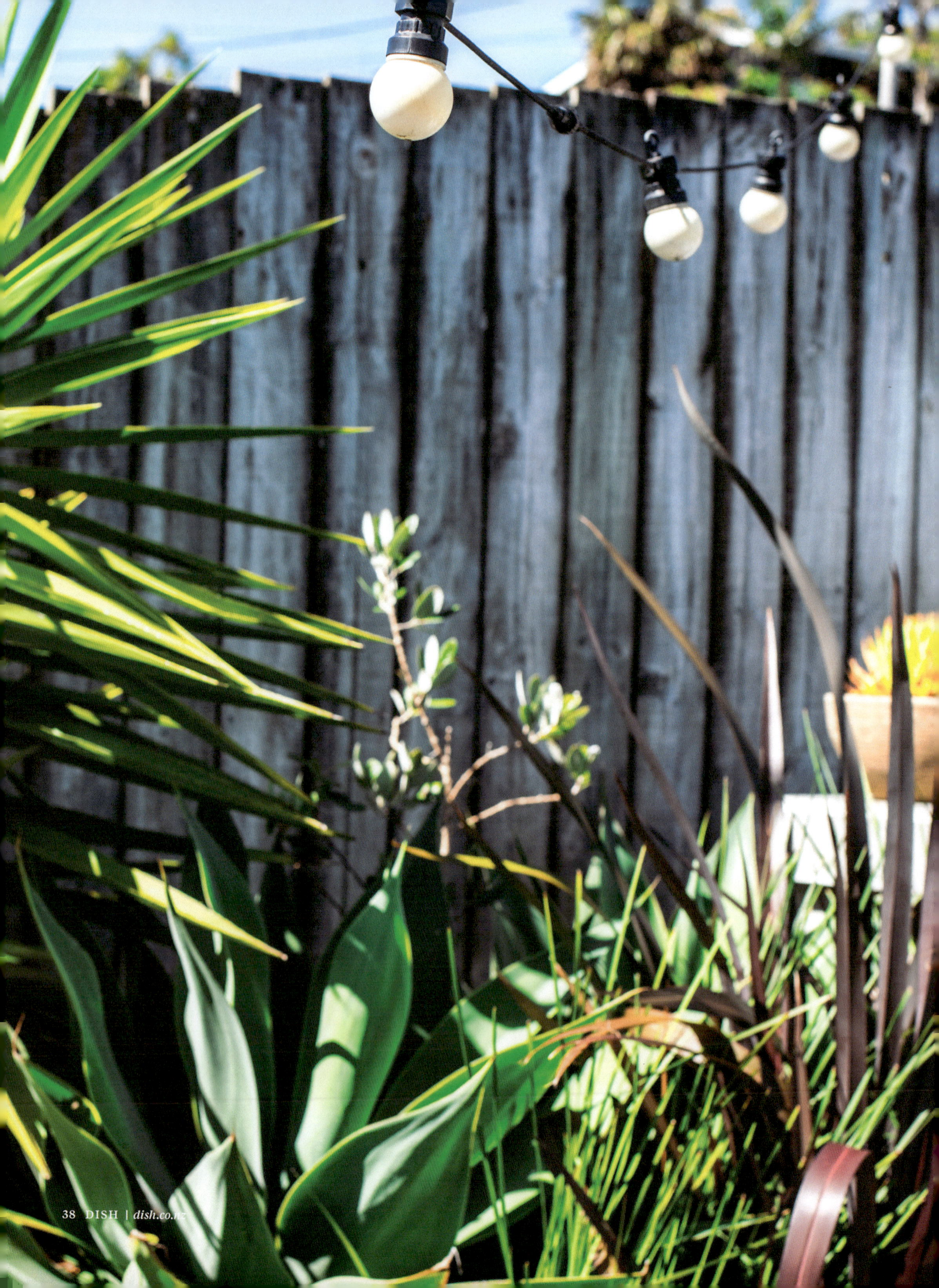

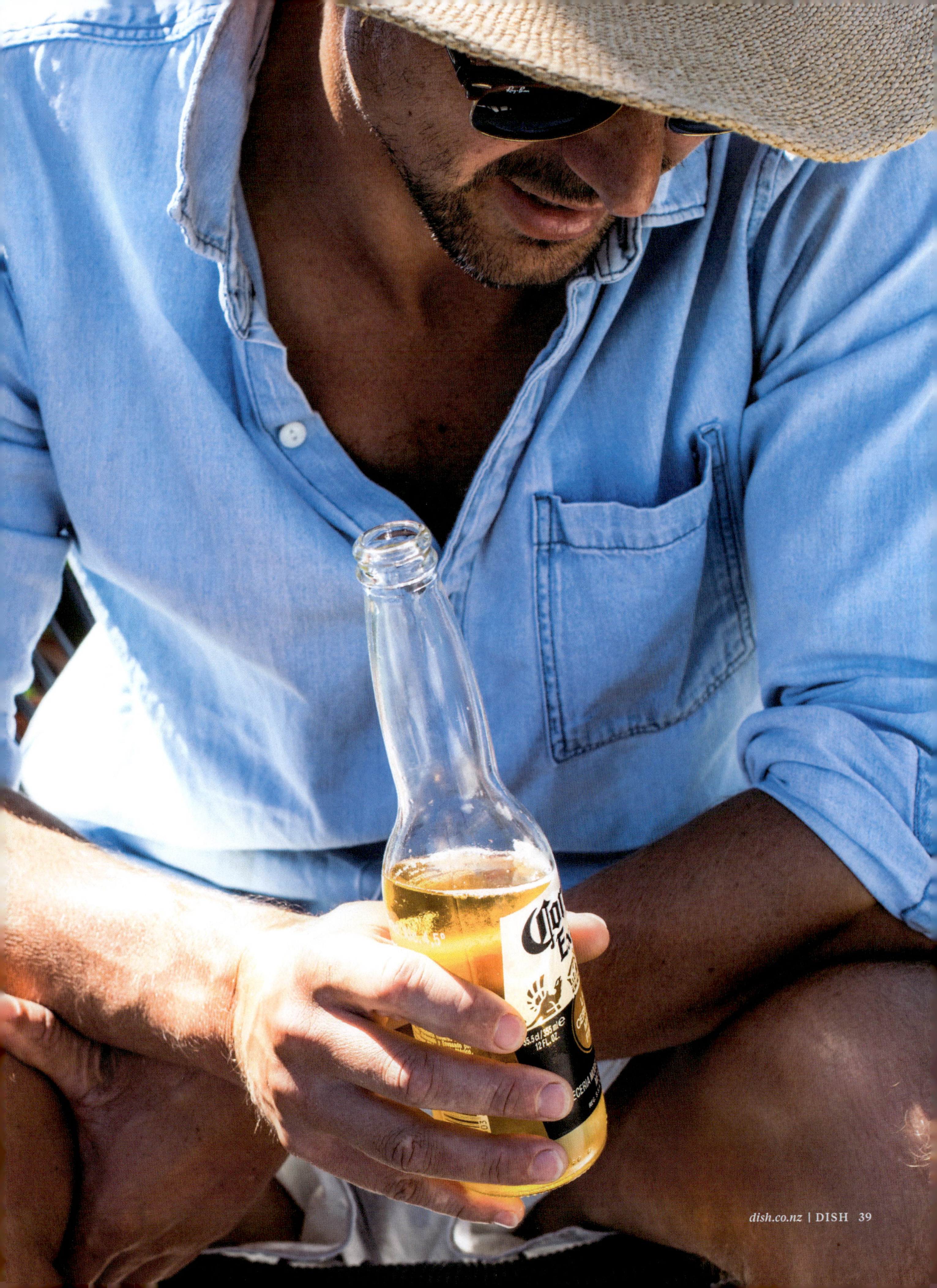

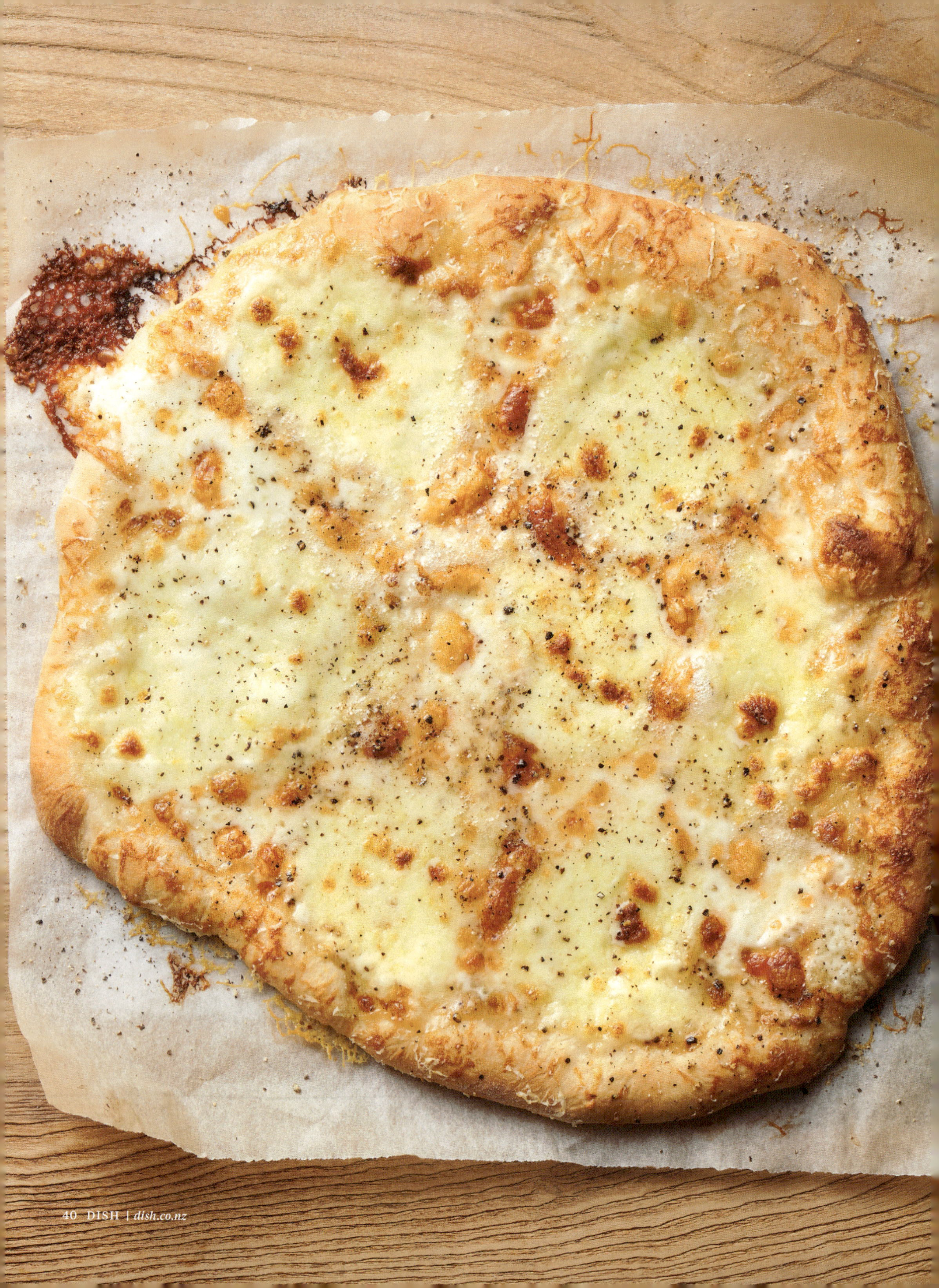

# Cacio e Pepe Pizza (v)

*Cacio e pepe is one of the simplest pasta dishes in Italian cuisine. We've taken the flavours and made it into a pizza bianca, a white pizza, plus added in a couple of extra cheeses to make it really sing.*

**MAKES 1 PIZZA**

½ portion Pizza Dough (see recipe page 215), or 1 purchased pizza base

1 tablespoon cream

1 cup freshly grated parmesan

125-gram ball fresh mozzarella in whey, well drained

125 grams taleggio, sliced

sea salt and black pepper

Preheat the oven to 225°C fan bake. Place a heavy, flat baking tray inside to preheat.

Roll out the dough on a large piece of baking paper to about 28cm. Brush the cream over the dough, then sprinkle with ½ cup parmesan. Rip the mozzarella into pieces and pat dry with kitchen towels. Dot over the pizza along with the taleggio, then sprinkle with the remaining ½ cup parmesan. Season with sea salt and grind over a generous amount of black pepper.

Slide the pizza, still on the paper, onto the hot baking tray and bake for about 12 minutes, or until puffed and golden, turning for even browning if necessary. Serve immediately.

# Mushroom and Caramelised Onion Pizza (v)

*We just about inhaled this pizza! With a delicious topping of rich caramelised onions, nutty mozzarella and earthy mushrooms, it smells as good as it looks.*

**MAKES 1 PIZZA**

½ portion Pizza Dough (see recipe page 215), or 1 purchased pizza base

olive oil, for brushing

¾ cup grated mozzarella

¾ cup Caramelised Onions (see recipe page 211)

250 grams button mushrooms, thinly sliced

sea salt and ground pepper

parmesan, for grating over

truffle oil for drizzling (optional)

1 tablespoon finely chopped parsley

Preheat the oven to 225°C fan bake. Place a heavy, flat baking tray inside to preheat.

Roll out the dough on a large piece of baking paper to about 28cm. Brush the dough with a little olive oil, then sprinkle over the mozzarella. Spread over the onions. Toss the mushrooms with a little olive oil and season generously. Scatter over the pizza, then grate over a generous amount of parmesan.

Slide the pizza, still on the paper, onto the hot baking tray and bake for about 12 minutes, or until puffed and golden, turning for even browning if necessary. Drizzle with a little truffle oil if using and sprinkle with parsley. Serve immediately.

dish.co.nz | DISH 43

# Spicy Salami, Prosciutto and Mozzarella Pizza

*Chilli salami and crispy prosciutto give this pizza a spicy, salty kick that sings with the peppery zip of rocket.*

**MAKES 1 PIZZA**

½ portion Pizza Dough (see recipe page 215), or 1 purchased pizza base

olive oil, for brushing

½ cup purchased tomato pasta sauce

½ cup freshly grated parmesan

80 grams thinly sliced calabrese salami

80 grams prosciutto

125-gram ball fresh mozzarella in whey, well drained

ground pepper

handful rocket leaves

Preheat the oven to 225°C fan bake. Place a heavy, flat baking tray inside to preheat.

Roll out the dough on a large piece of baking paper to about 28cm. Brush a 2cm border with olive oil, then spread the tomato sauce over the dough. Sprinkle over the parmesan and top with the salami and prosciutto. Rip the mozzarella into pieces and pat dry with kitchen towels. Dot over the pizza and drizzle with a little olive oil and a grind of pepper.

Slide the pizza, still on the paper, onto the hot baking tray and bake for about 12 minutes, or until puffed and golden, turning for even browning if necessary. Top with the rocket and serve immediately.

dish.co.nz | DISH 45

# Greens, Ricotta and Mushroom Pizza (v)

*The light, creamy herb and lemon ricotta base makes a nice change from the traditional 'red' pizza.*

**MAKES 1 PIZZA**

2 handfuls kale

olive oil, for massaging and brushing

sea salt and ground pepper

150 grams firm ricotta

finely grated zest 1 lemon

2 cloves garlic, crushed

1 teaspoon chopped thyme leaves

½ portion Pizza Dough (see recipe page 215), or 1 purchased pizza base

100 grams mushrooms (I used oyster mushrooms but you can use button or portobello; just slice thinly before using)

parmesan, for grating over

Preheat the oven to 225°C fan bake. Place a heavy, flat baking tray inside to preheat.

Put the kale in a heatproof bowl and cover with boiling water. Leave for 5 minutes, then drain and refresh under cold water. Roll up in a clean tea towel and squeeze out all the water. Roughly chop, then massage with a little olive oil, salt and pepper. Combine the ricotta, lemon zest, garlic and thyme and season with salt and pepper.

Roll out the dough on a large piece of baking paper to about 28cm. Brush the dough with olive oil, then spread with the ricotta mixture, leaving a border. Dot over the kale, then rip the mushrooms and place on top. Brush with oil and salt. Slide the pizza, still on the paper, onto the hot baking tray and bake for 12 minutes, or until puffed and golden, turning for even browning if necessary.

Top with a good grating of parmesan and serve immediately.

**COOK'S NOTE:** Strip the kale leaves off the stalks before measuring.

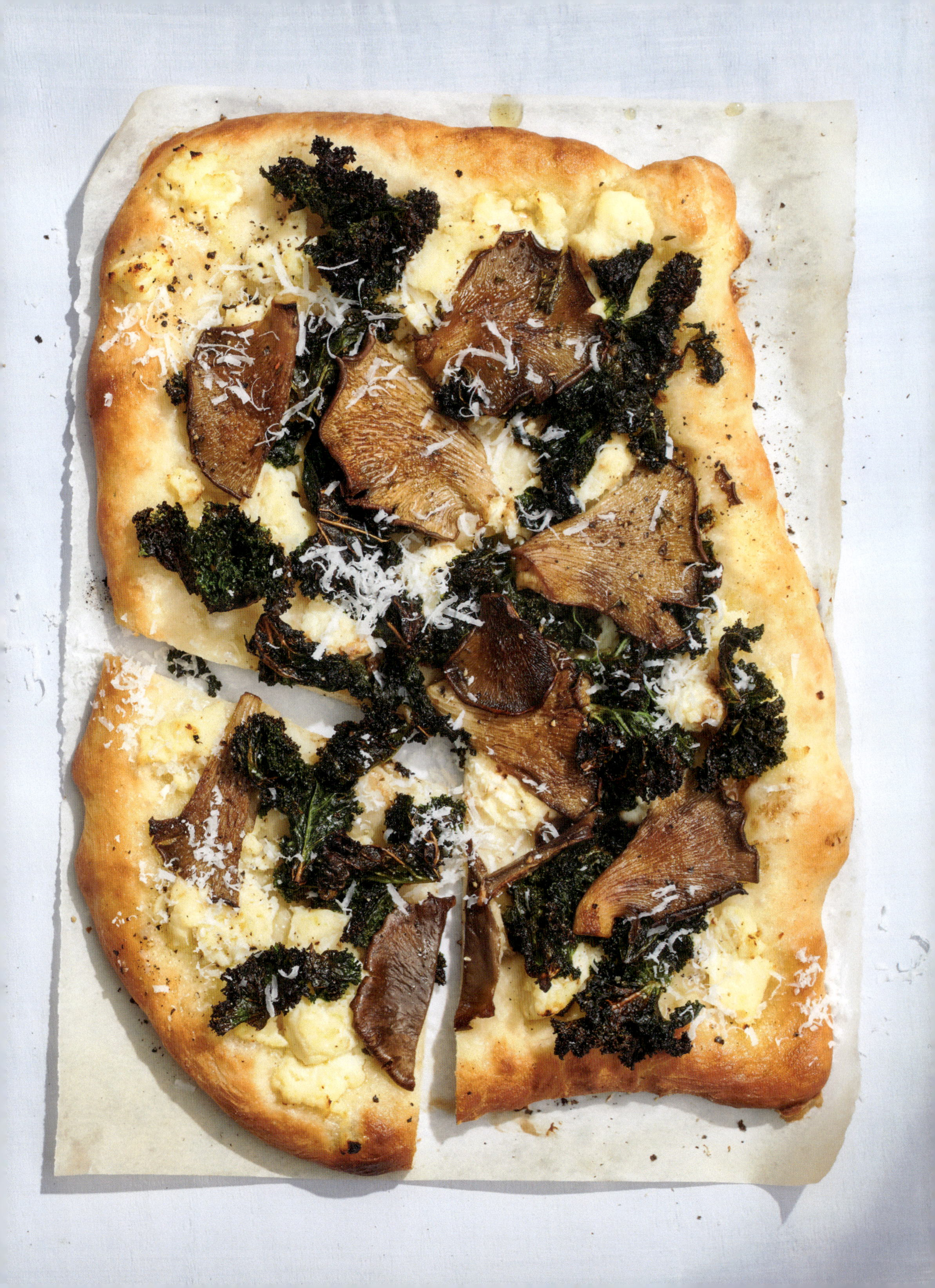

# Fresh Fennel, Salami and Chilli Pizza

*A hit of aniseed from the fennel pairs beautifully with good salami, a kick of chilli and rich molten cheese.*

**MAKES 1 PIZZA**

½ portion Pizza Dough (see recipe page 215), or 1 purchased pizza base

olive oil, for brushing

½ cup thick tomato pasta sauce (I used Telegraph Hill Puttanesca Sauce)

80 grams thinly sliced salami

1 small fennel bulb, top trimmed, fronds reserved, sliced

100 grams melting cheese, such as stracchino, mozzarella or fontina

chilli flakes or chopped fresh chilli

Preheat the oven to 225°C fan bake. Place a heavy, flat baking tray inside to preheat.

Roll out the dough on a large piece of baking paper to about 28cm. Brush the dough with a little olive oil, then spread with the tomato sauce, leaving a border around the edge. Lay the salami over the top. Toss the fennel slices with a little olive oil and arrange on top, then dot over the cheese.

Slide the pizza, still on the paper, onto the hot baking tray and bake for about 12 minutes, or until puffed and golden, turning for even browning if necessary.

Scatter over chilli flakes to taste, then the reserved fennel fronds, if desired. Serve immediately.

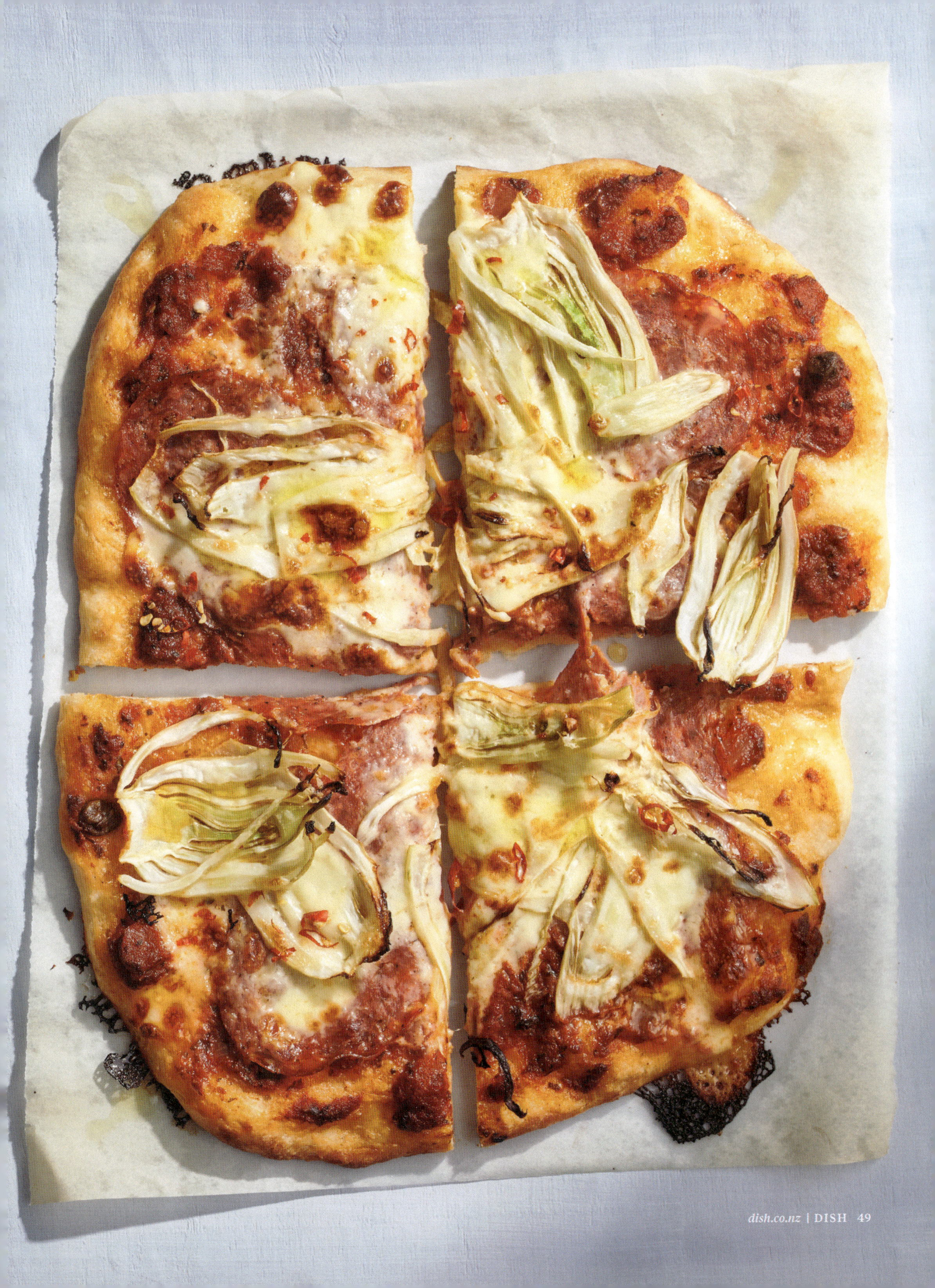

# Baked Tomatoes and Spaghetti (v)

*This simple baked topping is a gorgeous mélange of juicy tomatoes, salty olives, sweet citrus and a hint of chilli.*

**SERVES 2**

**BAKED TOMATOES**
400 grams mixed cherry tomatoes, halved

8 black olives

2 cloves garlic, crushed

chilli flakes, to taste

2 tablespoons olive oil, plus extra to serve

1 teaspoon dried oregano

finely grated zest and juice ½ orange and ½ lemon

**TO SERVE**
200 grams dried spaghetti

125-gram ball fresh mozzarella in whey, well drained

basil

Preheat the oven to 190°C fan bake.

**BAKED TOMATOES:** Put all the ingredients in a large bowl and combine well. Tip into a large overproof frying pan or shallow baking dish.

Roast for about 20 minutes, or until the tomatoes are well-coloured and starting to collapse.

While the tomatoes are cooking, cook the pasta according to the packet instructions and drain.

**TO SERVE:** Place the hot spaghetti in the pan alongside the tomatoes. Rip over the mozzarella and top with a grind of pepper, some basil leaves and a drizzle of olive oil.

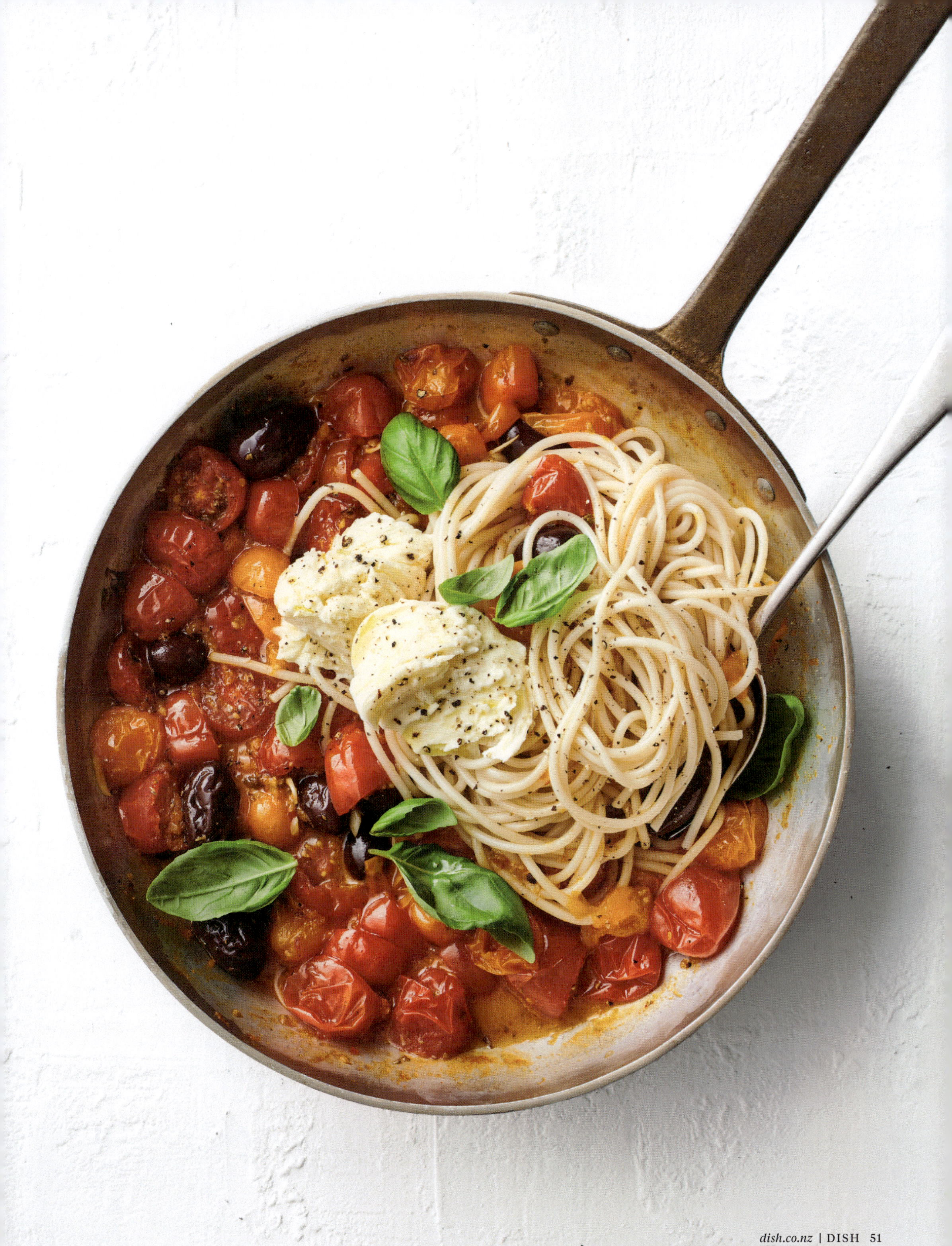

# Chilli Prawn Pasta

*Ready in a flash, this pasta with a kick is the perfect laid-back summer meal solution.*

**SERVES 4**

1 tablespoon olive oil

120 grams pancetta or streaky bacon, chopped

5 mini sweet capsicums, sliced

24 raw prawn cutlets

2 red chillies, sliced

4 cloves garlic, crushed

2 x 400-gram tins whole cherry tomatoes

2 tablespoons tomato paste

420 grams dried linguine or spaghetti

Heat the olive oil in a large frying pan and add the pancetta. Cook for 3-4 minutes, until starting to get crispy, then add the capsicums. Cook, stirring, for 1 minute, then add the prawns, chillies and garlic. Cook for 3-4 minutes, turning the prawns once. Add the cherry tomatoes and their juice and the tomato paste and stir to combine. Cook together for 5 minutes.

While the sauce is cooking, cook the pasta according to the packet instructions and drain, reserving 2 tablespoons of the cooking water.

Add the drained pasta and cooking water to the prawn mixture and stir to combine. Serve immediately.

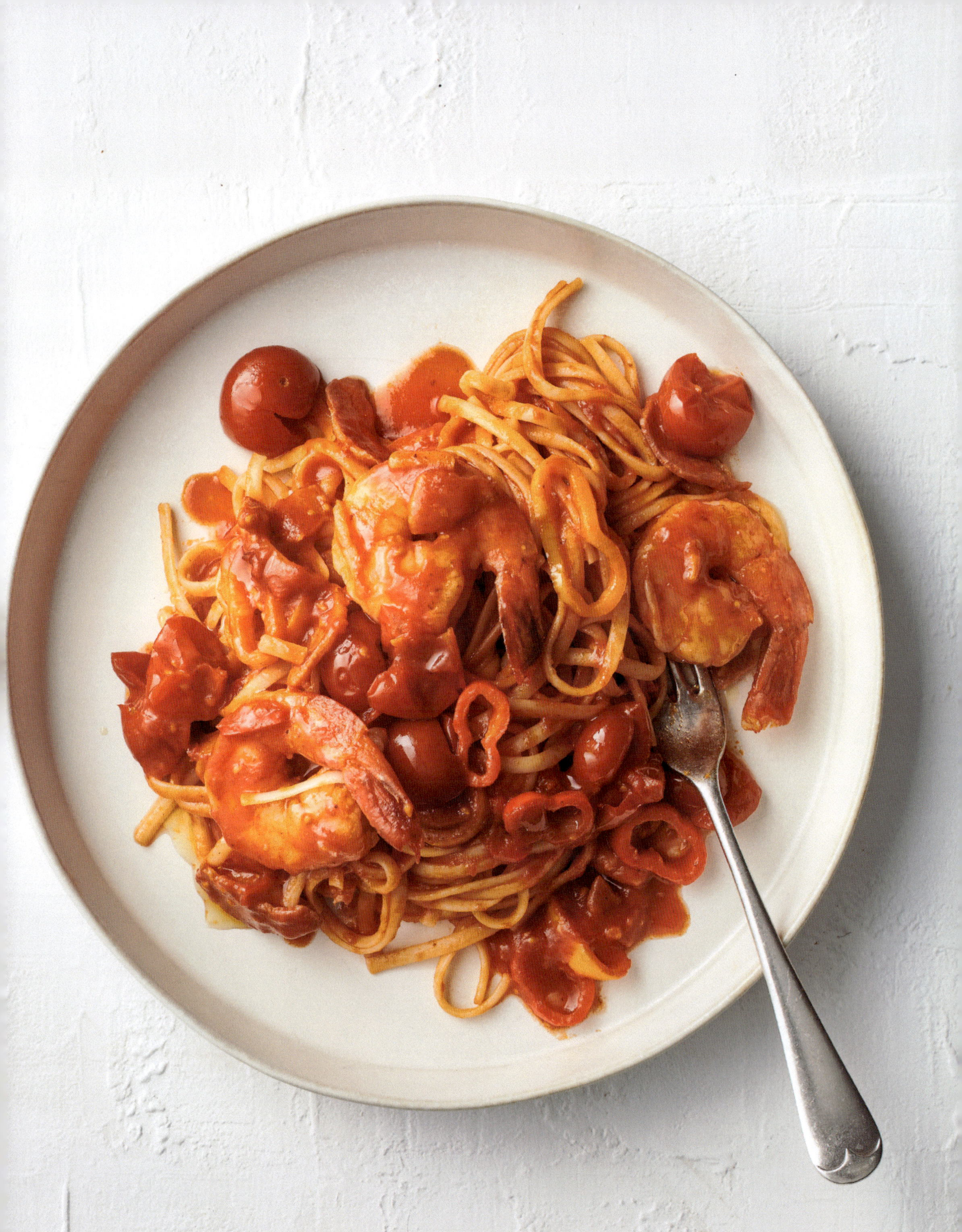

# Market Fish with Green Olive, Jalapeño and Tomato Salsa (gf)

*You can use any fish for this recipe – whatever is fresh and best on the day. Jalapeños add quite a kick to the salsa, so use less if you prefer it milder.*

**SERVES 4-6**

750 grams fish fillets

2 teaspoons cumin seeds

sea salt and ground pepper

2 tablespoons olive oil

**SALSA**
¼ cup olive oil

2 tablespoons lemon juice

2 cloves garlic, crushed

1 teaspoon cumin seeds, toasted

2 medium tomatoes, diced

2 spring onions, sliced thinly

10 pitted green olives, chopped roughly

2 tablespoons sliced jalapeños in brine, drained

Sprinkle both sides of the fish with cumin seeds, salt and pepper. Preheat a barbecue flat plate, or large frying pan, to medium and brush lightly with oil. Cook the fish until just cooked through. *Cooking time will depend on the thickness of the fillets.*

**SALSA:** Whisk the oil, lemon juice, garlic and cumin seeds in a bowl and season. Stir in the remaining ingredients.

**TO SERVE:** Place the fish on plates and spoon over the salsa.

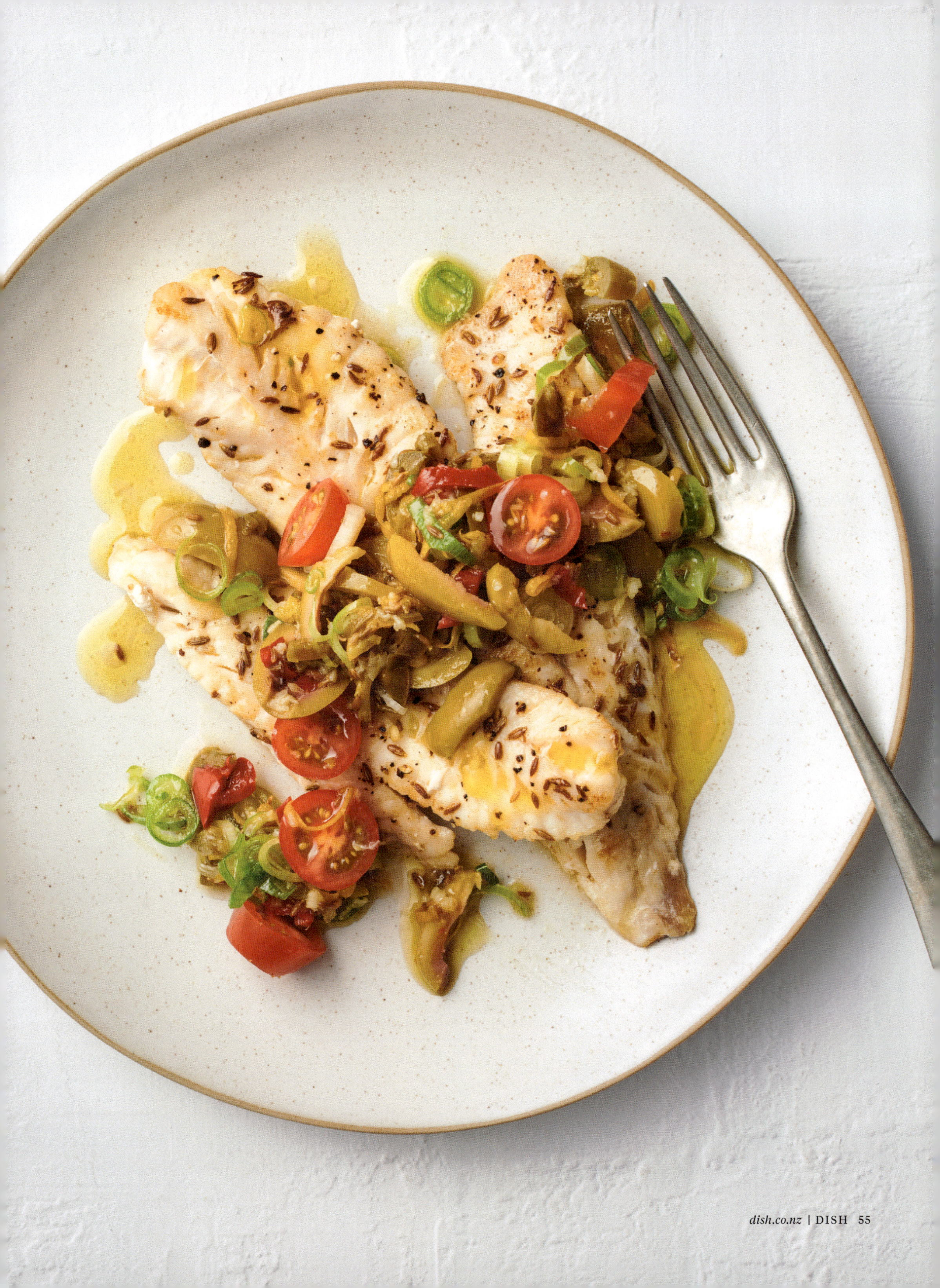

# Baked Prawns with Lemon and Feta (gf)

*This is the perfect dish to serve with lots of crusty bread for mopping up all the lovely garlicky, lemony juices.*

**SERVES 2**

10 large raw, peeled prawns, tail on

2 medium vine tomatoes, roughly chopped

zest and juice 1 lemon

¼ cup olive oil

2 cloves garlic, crushed

pinch chilli flakes

1 teaspoon dried oregano, preferably Sicilian

sea salt and ground pepper

125 grams firm feta cheese, broken into large pieces

1 tablespoon chopped parsley

Preheat the oven to 200°C fan bake.

Toss the prawns with all the ingredients except the feta. Tip into a medium-sized, shallow, ovenproof baking dish. Nestle the feta pieces into the dish and spoon over some of the juices and a grind of pepper.

Bake for 15 minutes, until the prawns are just cooked. Scatter over the parsley and serve.

dish.co.nz | DISH 57

# Roast Salmon with Pomegranate Glaze and Herby Yoghurt Mayo (gf)

*Even non-salmon lovers can't resist this dish. Not too oily, glazed in tangy pomegranate molasses, just cooked and with a side of sharp quick-pickled red onion and a dollop of herby yoghurt mayo, it is a total winner.*

**SERVES 8-10**

**QUICK-PICKLED ONION**

⅓ cup cider vinegar

1 tablespoon caster sugar

1 small red onion, finely sliced

**SALMON**

2 tablespoons extra-virgin olive oil

3 garlic cloves, crushed

1½ tablespoons pomegranate molasses

1 teaspoon cumin seeds, lightly crushed

2 tablespoons sea salt

½ cup boiling water

5½ cups cold water

1.5-kilogram (approx.) side of salmon

dill fronds, to garnish

Herby Yoghurt Mayo (recipe page 212)

**QUICK-PICKLED ONION:** Put the vinegar and sugar in a small, non-reactive bowl and whisk to dissolve the sugar. Add the onion, cover and refrigerate until ready to serve.

**SALMON:** Mix the olive oil with the garlic, pomegranate molasses and cumin seeds in a small bowl. Set aside.

Put the salt in a big roasting dish, deep enough to lay the salmon in, and with capacity for 6 cups of water. Add the ½ cup boiling water to the salt and whisk to dissolve. Top up with the 5½ cups of cold water and leave to cool.

Once cold, add the salmon, flesh side down, and leave in the brine for 30 minutes. *This will help to prevent the milky white fat from rising to the top of the salmon while cooking.*

Preheat the oven to 230°C regular bake and line an oven tray with baking paper.

Remove the salmon from the brine and pat dry. Lay skin-side down on the baking tray and brush with the olive oil mixture. Bake for 10-15 minutes. *I did 15 minutes for my 1.5-kilogram piece, but if your salmon is smaller, stick to 12 minutes or less – you really don't want to overcook it.*

Once cooked, the salmon can be served immediately or refrigerated until half an hour before serving. When ready to serve, garnish with dill fronds and the drained onion and serve with the mayo, topped with extra capers and dill fronds.

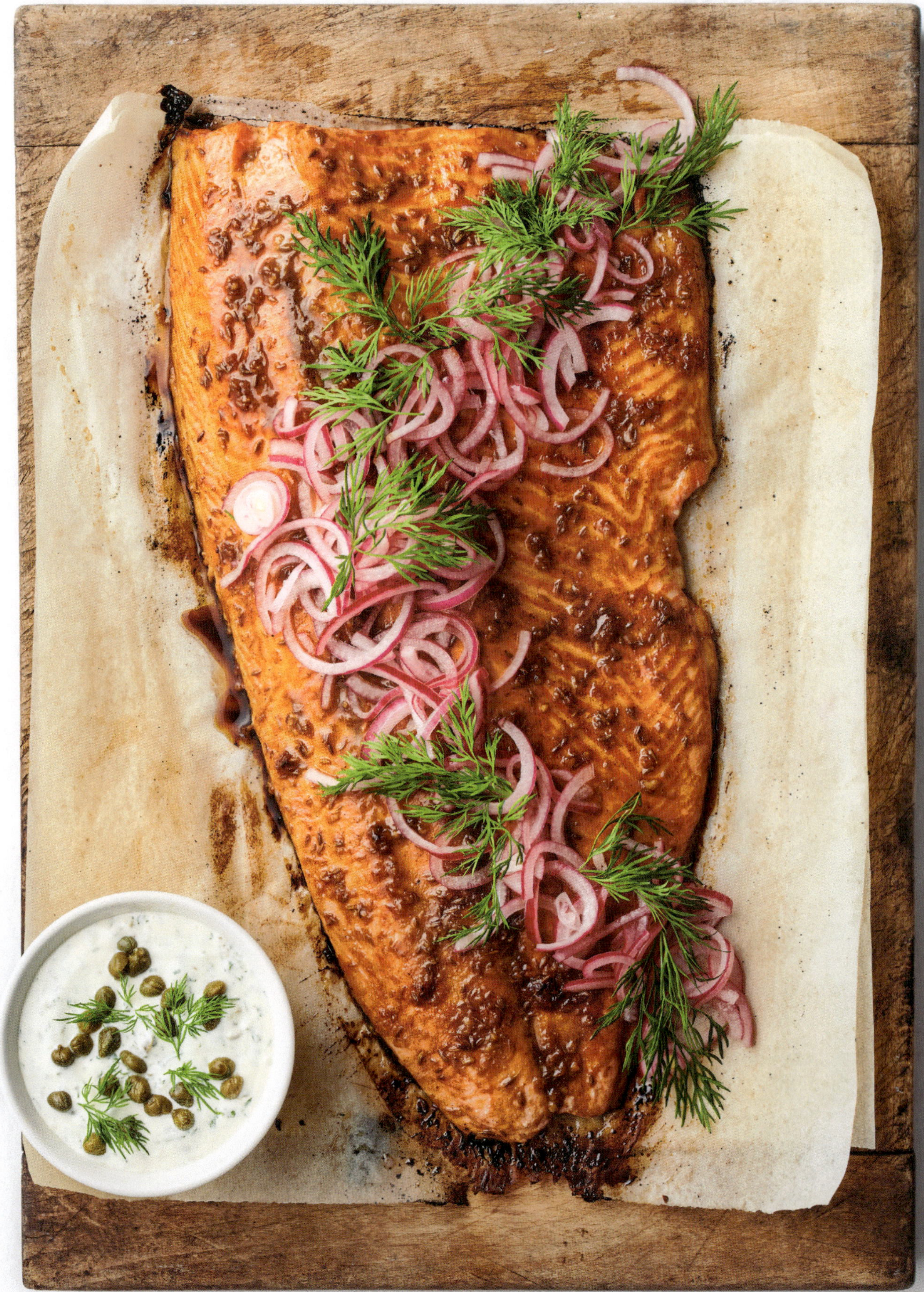

# Best-ever Fresh Catch Beer-battered Fish

*'Best-ever' is a slightly overused term these days and not one we use lightly. BUT, this recipe certainly deserves that claim to fame. The secret is to have really cold flour and beer. I keep the flour in the freezer, weighed up in small bags, ready to be whipped out to make this perfectly crunchy and totally delicious battered fish.*

**SERVES 4-6**

1 litre neutral oil, for frying

1 tablespoon baking powder

1 teaspoon sea salt

1¼ cups plain flour, well chilled

250ml very cold lager

600 grams firm white fish, cut into serving portions

**TO SERVE**

Chips (see recipe below)

lemon wedges

Tartare Sauce (see recipe page 218)

Heat the oil in a deep saucepan to 180°C, or until a piece of bread dropped in turns golden in 30 seconds.

Whisk the baking powder and salt into the chilled flour. Quickly whisk in the cold beer until you have a thick batter. *Do all of this just before you cook the fish.*

Dip your fish into the batter, then, holding it on the slimmer end, very slowly lower it into the oil so the batter starts to instantly puff up, before lowering it fully into the pan. *If you let go straight away it will sink to the bottom and stick on the base of the pan.*

The fish will take about 2 minutes each side to cook, but this will depend on the thickness of the fillets. Remove and drain on kitchen towels. Sprinkle with a little sea salt and keep warm on a cooling rack set over a baking tray in a low oven while you cook the remaining fish.

**TO SERVE:** Serve the fish with Chips, lemon wedges for squeezing over and Tartare Sauce.

# Chips (gf) (v)

**SERVES 4**

6 large Agria potatoes

neutral oil, for cooking

sea salt

Peel and cut the potatoes into chips, then place in a large saucepan of salted water. Bring to the boil, then cook until the chips have started to soften. Carefully drain and set aside to cool. *This can be done well ahead of time.* Heat 1cm oil in a large frying pan and cook the chips until golden, tender on the inside and crisp on the outside. Drain on kitchen towels and sprinkle with sea salt.

dish.co.nz | DISH 61

# Baked Spanish Rice with Chicken and Chorizo (gf)

*Who doesn't like a tray bake? It's a classic that will have the whole family going back for seconds.*

**SERVES 4-6**

2 tablespoons olive oil

6 small chicken thighs, skin on, bone in

4 chicken drumsticks

1 onion, diced

3 cloves garlic, crushed

2 teaspoons smoked paprika

1 tablespoon finely chopped rosemary

sea salt and ground pepper

200 grams gluten-free chorizo, sliced into 1cm pieces

1 cup calasparra or arborio rice

3½ cups chicken stock

400-gram tin whole cherry tomatoes

2 tablespoons finely chopped fresh parsley, to serve

Preheat the oven to 180°C fan bake.

Heat the oil in a large frying pan and brown the chicken on all sides, then set aside. *Don't wash the pan.*

Add the onion, garlic, paprika and rosemary to the pan with a good pinch of salt and cook for 5 minutes. Stir in the chorizo, rice, stock and tomatoes. Season and bring to the boil.

Tip into a large roasting dish and nestle in the chicken. Cover with foil and bake for 20 minutes. Uncover and bake for a further 20 minutes, or until the chicken is fully cooked. Top with parsley before serving.

dish.co.nz | DISH 63

# Lemongrass and Garlic Roasted Pork Belly

*This fragrant pork is incredibly tender and juicy. Add in the crispy crackling and you'll be in porkie heaven.*

**SERVES 4-6**

**PASTE**
1 large stalk lemongrass, grated on a fine microplane

1 tablespoon grated fresh ginger

2 cloves garlic, crushed

2 tablespoons vegetable oil

**PORK**
1.3-kilogram piece boneless pork belly, skin on

sea salt

vegetable oil

1 cup coconut cream

½ cup water

**TO SERVE**
Pineapple Sambal (see recipe page 214)

Soy and Lime Dipping Sauce (see recipe page 217)

Preheat the oven to 225°C fan bake.

**PASTE:** Stir all the ingredients together.

**PORK:** Lightly score the flesh side of the pork. Season with salt and rub in the paste. Make a basket of foil in a baking dish, slightly larger than the piece of pork, and place the pork in it, skin-side up. Brush the skin with oil and sprinkle with sea salt.

Combine the coconut cream and water and pour into the foil basket to come halfway up the flesh. *Don't pour it over the skin.* Reserve any remaining liquid for adding later. Roast for 30 minutes.

Reduce the heat to 160°C regular bake. Cook for 1 hour more, or until the pork is very tender when pierced with a skewer. Add more liquid to the pan as needed. *Don't let the liquid evaporate entirely as this keeps the meat very tender.* If, at the end of the cooking time, the skin hasn't crackled enough, place under a hot grill for a few minutes, taking care it doesn't catch and burn.

**TO SERVE:** Place the pork on a platter. Serve with Pineapple Sambal and Soy and Lime Dipping Sauce.

dish.co.nz | DISH 65

# FIRE UP THE BARBIE

*We love a quintessential Kiwi barbecue – even a classic grilled sausage in white bread with tomato sauce on a hot day hits the spot. Here we elevate the regular offerings with stunning options such as Grilled Corn with Whipped Ricotta and Smoky Chilli Butter (page 78), Sticky Tamarind and Maple Syrup Glazed Pork Ribs (page 72), and the new classic, Beer Can Chicken with White Barbecue Sauce (page 88). There is something so liberating about cooking alfresco and gathering friends to enjoy the early evening sun. Time to dust off the barbie, break out the tongs and get cracking!*

dish.co.nz | DISH 67

68 DISH | dish.co.nz

dish.co.nz | DISH 69

# Grilled Zucchini with Tzatziki and Kasundi (gf) (v)

*This simple but delicious recipe is all about the accompaniments that you need to lavishly pile on top of the grilled zucchini.*

**SERVES 4**

8 medium zucchini

olive oil, for brushing

sea salt and ground pepper

200 grams purchased tzatziki

½ cup purchased kasundi (see Cook's note)

2 tablespoons purchased dukkah

small mint leaves, to garnish

Preheat a ridged grill plate or a barbecue to medium.

Using a vegetable peeler, take a strip of skin off both sides of each zucchini so they will lie flat. Brush with oil and season with salt and pepper.

Cook on the grill, turning occasionally, until just tender but not totally soft when pierced with a skewer, and lightly charred on the outside. Set aside to cool.

**TO SERVE:** Cut down the centre of each zucchini to split open a little. Place on a serving plate, top with dollops of tzatziki and kasundi and sprinkle with dukkah. Garnish with mint leaves.

**COOK'S NOTE:** Kasundi is a tomato-based Indian spiced relish and can be found in the condiment aisle at good food stores and supermarkets.

dish.co.nz | DISH 71

# Sticky Tamarind and Maple Syrup Glazed Pork Ribs

*Apart from being super delicious, what I love about ribs is that both the ribs and the glaze can be prepared in advance then just finished off on the barbecue for a finger-licking feast.*

**SERVES 6**

**RIBS**
3 x 500-gram racks pork spare ribs

sea salt

1 cup hot water

**GLAZE**
⅔ cup maple syrup

½ cup kecap manis

¼ cup oyster sauce

¼ cup black vinegar (Chinkiang vinegar)

2 tablespoons tamarind concentrate

2 tablespoons sriracha chilli sauce

1 teaspoon ground cinnamon

1 teaspoon sea salt

**TO COOK AND SERVE**
lime wedges, for squeezing over

Preheat the oven to 180°C fan bake.

**RIBS:** Use a sharp knife to cut loose one edge of the skin, which is the thin membrane on the bone side of the ribs. Grab the edge with a kitchen towel then pull off the entire skin and discard. Season the ribs with salt then place in a large baking dish. Pour in the water and cover with baking paper then foil to seal tightly. Bake for 1 hour. Remove and pat dry with kitchen towels.

**GLAZE:** Place all the ingredients in a medium saucepan and bring to the boil. Reduce the heat and simmer for 5 minutes. Cool. Tip half of the glaze into a serving bowl and set aside for serving.

**TO COOK AND SERVE:** Preheat the barbecue or a grill plate to medium-low.

Brush the ribs with some of the remaining glaze and place over the heat. Turn and brush the ribs every 5 minutes until golden and sticky, about 15 minutes. *Don't have the heat too hot or the glaze will quickly catch and burn.*

Transfer to a serving board and serve with the reserved glaze for dipping and lime wedges for squeezing.

**COOK'S NOTE:** The glaze can be made several days ahead, and the ribs can be baked 3 days ahead of glazing. Store both in the fridge.

dish.co.nz | DISH 73

# Sausage Coil with Charred Broccolini and Avocado and Olive Salsa (gf)

*Use your favourite sausages and serve alongside the charred broccolini and salsa if a coil isn't available.*

**SERVES 4-6**

1 long coiled sausage (see Cook's note)

250 grams broccolini, cut in half lengthways

olive oil

sea salt and ground pepper

**SALSA**
finely grated zest 1 lime

1 tablespoon lime juice

1 tablespoon olive oil

3 medium vine tomatoes, halved, seeds removed and roughly chopped

10 black olives, pitted and roughly chopped

¼ packed cup small parsley leaves

**TO SERVE**
1 avocado, sliced

Push long, thin skewers through the sausage to keep it together when cooking. Grill on a preheated barbecue until cooked through, turning once.

Toss the broccolini with oil, salt and pepper and cook on the barbecue for a few minutes until lightly charred and bright green.

**SALSA:** Combine all the ingredients in a bowl and season.

**TO SERVE:** Remove the skewers and place the sausage on a serving platter. Top with the broccolini, avocado and salsa.

**COOK'S NOTE:** I used a tasty Boerewors sausage from South Africa. With a bit of notice, your butcher will generally make a long coil of your favourite sausage for you. Pork and fennel seed would also be delicious.

dish.co.nz | DISH 75

# Haloumi and Peach Kebabs (gf) (v)

*These salty/sweet kebabs are simple to put together and get an added boost from the honey, crunchy dukkah and chilli flakes.*

**MAKES 8 KEBABS**

2 x 200-gram packets haloumi, each cut into 8 chunks

2 peaches, each cut into 8 chunks

olive oil

sea salt and ground pepper

**TO SERVE**
½ cup thick plain yoghurt (optional)

honey or maple syrup, chilli flakes, dukkah and fresh baby basil leaves

warm flatbreads (optional)

**EQUIPMENT:** 8 x 20cm thin metal skewers or wooden skewers soaked in water for 1 hour.

Thread the haloumi and peaches onto 8 skewers. Brush with oil and season with salt and pepper. Cook on the barbecue grill for 2-3 minutes each side, until the cheese is golden and the peaches begin to lightly char.

**TO SERVE:** Spread the yoghurt over the base of a serving platter, if using. Top with the kebabs, drizzle with honey or maple syrup and sprinkle with chilli flakes, dukkah and baby basil leaves. Serve with flatbreads, if desired.

# Lamb and Bacon-wrapped Date Kebabs (gf)

*Juicy chunks of spicy lamb, crispy bacon and warm dates equals kebab heaven.*

**MAKES 8 KEBABS**

4 lamb shortloins, each sliced into 8 pieces

sea salt

1 tablespoon ras el hanout (Moroccan spice rub)

16 dates, pitted

5-6 strips streaky bacon

**TO SERVE**
1 cup thick plain yoghurt

Herb and Pistachio Dressing (see recipe 212)

¼ cup chopped pistachios

**EQUIPMENT:** 8 x 20cm thin metal skewers or wooden skewers soaked in water for 1 hour.

Season the lamb with salt then toss with the ras el hanout. Wrap each date in a strip of bacon. Thread the lamb and dates onto the skewers. *Don't push the meat and dates tightly together.* Cook the kebabs on the barbecue grill over a high heat for 2 minutes on each side, or until the lamb is cooked to your liking.

**TO SERVE:** Spread the yoghurt on a platter. Arrange the kebabs on top, spoon over the dressing and scatter with pistachios.

dish.co.nz | DISH | 77

# Grilled Corn with Whipped Ricotta and Smoky Chilli Butter (gf) (v)

*I had this stunning combination at Fonda, my favourite Mexican eatery and bar in Parnell. Whipped ricotta is now my go-to topping and I make a simple smoky butter to pour over the top. You can also serve the ricotta and smoky butter in separate bowls.*

**SERVES 4**

4 ears corn on the cob

2 teaspoons olive oil

250 grams ricotta, well drained

2 teaspoons sea salt, plus extra to serve

2-3 tablespoons milk

**SMOKY CHILLI BUTTER**
100 grams butter

1 teaspoon each smoked paprika, chilli flakes and sea salt

½-1 teaspoon chilli powder, plus extra to serve

**TO SERVE**
parmesan, for grating over

Cook the corn in plenty of salted boiling water until just tender. Drain well and break each cob in half.

Heat the oil on a barbecue hot plate on high. Add the corn and cook until lightly charred in places.

Beat the ricotta and salt with enough milk until light in texture.

**SMOKY CHILLI BUTTER:** Place all the ingredients in a small saucepan. Cook on the preheated barbecue hot plate for 5 minutes, stirring often so it doesn't catch on the base of the pan, until the butter is lightly browned and has a gorgeous nutty aroma. Tip into a bowl.

**TO SERVE:** Pile the corn up on a platter and top with a generous grating of parmesan and a pinch of chilli powder and sea salt. Spoon the ricotta into a mound and make a hollow in the centre, then pour in the butter. Serve immediately.

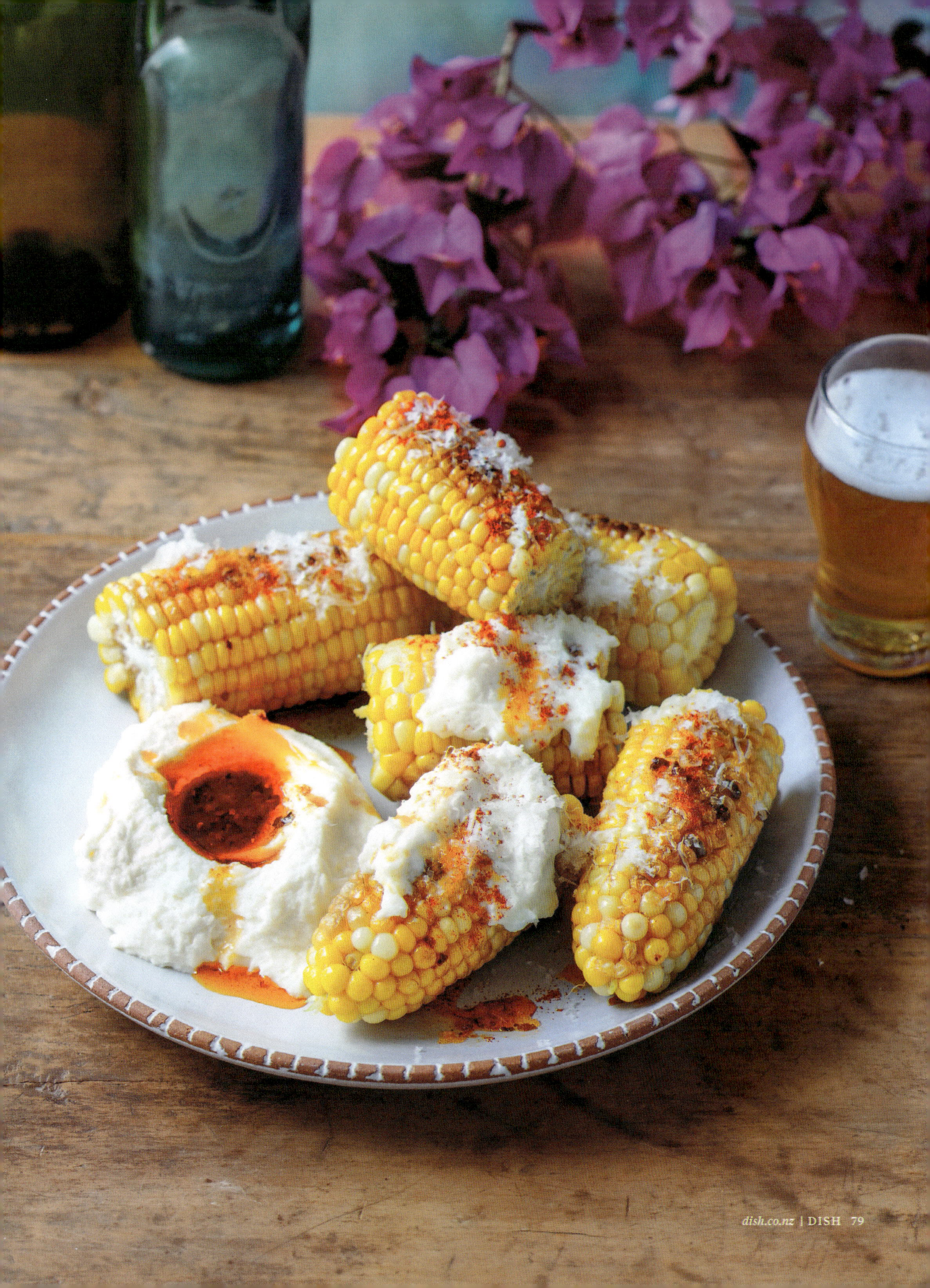

# Chipotle Prawns with Lime and Jalapeño Mayo (gf)

*Make sure the heat isn't too hot or the chipotle paste will catch and burn.*

**SERVES 4**

**CHIPOTLE PASTE**
2 chipotle peppers in adobo sauce

1 teaspoon each adobo sauce, paprika, cumin and sea salt

2 cloves garlic, crushed

1 tablespoon apple cider vinegar

2 tablespoons olive oil

**TO COOK AND SERVE**
20 large, peeled raw prawns, tails on

vegetable oil, for cooking

lime wedges

Lime and Jalapeño Mayo (see recipe below)

**CHIPOTLE PASTE:** Place all the ingredients in a small food processor and blend until smooth.

**TO COOK AND SERVE:** Put the prawns in a large bowl and toss with the chipotle paste, turning to coat well.

Heat 2 tablespoons oil on a barbecue hot plate on medium-low and cook the prawns until golden. *Do this in two batches if needed, adding more oil as needed.*

Pile the prawns up in a dish and serve with the lime wedges and Lime and Jalapeño Mayo.

# Lime and Jalapeño Mayo (gf)(v)

**MAKES ABOUT 1 CUP**

½ cup each sour cream and mayonnaise

1 tablespoon sliced jalapeños in brine, drained and finely chopped, plus extra for garnish

finely grated zest 1 lime

2 tablespoons lime juice

2 cloves garlic, crushed

1 teaspoon sea salt

Whisk all the ingredients together and top with extra sliced jalapeños to serve.

dish.co.nz | DISH 81

# Steak Tacos with Charred Pineapple Salsa

*Taco Tuesday – or any other day! Sure, they're a bit messy to eat but oh so delicious. Just serve with lots of big napkins.*

**MAKES 8 TACOS**

600 grams sirloin steak

2 tablespoons purchased Mexican spice blend

2 teaspoons olive oil

**TO ASSEMBLE**

8 tortillas, warmed

good-quality egg mayonnaise (see Cook's note)

big handful salad leaves

1-2 avocados, sliced

Charred Pineapple Salsa (see recipe below)

100 grams feta

fresh coriander

lime wedges

Sprinkle both sides of the steaks with the spice blend.

Heat the oil on a barbecue hot plate and cook the steaks for 2-3 minutes each side for medium-rare. *Cooking time will depend on the thickness of the steak.* Transfer to a plate to rest for a few minutes.

**TO ASSEMBLE:** Slice the steaks thinly against the grain. Spread the tortillas with mayo, if using, then top with salad leaves, steak, avocado, salsa, crumbled feta and coriander. Serve with lime wedges for squeezing over the top.

**COOK'S NOTE:** I spread the tortillas with the Lime and Jalapeño Mayo from page 80 for an extra layer of deliciousness.

# Charred Pineapple Salsa (gf) (v)

**MAKES ABOUT 2 CUPS**

½ fresh pineapple, skin removed, cut into 2cm-thick rounds

2 tablespoons lime juice

1 teaspoon sea salt

1 small red onion, thinly sliced

3 tablespoons olive oil

2 long green chillies, thinly sliced

2 spring onions, thinly sliced

Heat a barbecue hot plate on high and cook the pineapple for a few minutes each side, until lightly charred in places. Cool, then cut into 1cm pieces, discarding the core.

Combine the lime juice, salt and red onion in a large bowl and leave for 5 minutes. Stir in the oil, chillies, spring onions and pineapple.

dish.co.nz | DISH 83

# Grilled Steak Sandwich with Caramelised Onions and Mushrooms

*If you want a vegetarian version, slices of grilled haloumi with tomato relish will go perfectly with the sticky onions and mushrooms.*

**MAKES 4**

2 large brown onions, thinly sliced

2 tablespoons each olive oil and butter

sea salt and ground pepper

2 cloves garlic, crushed

2 teaspoons finely chopped rosemary or thyme

6 large portobello mushrooms, sliced

1 tablespoon soy sauce

2 x 200-gram rib eye steaks or sirloin steaks

**TO SERVE**
4 ciabatta rolls, warmed, halved, buttered

good-quality egg mayonnaise

rocket leaves

mustard

Cook the onions with the oil and butter and a good pinch of salt on a barbecue hot plate until soft. Add the garlic, herbs and mushrooms and continue to cook, turning often, until tender. Sprinkle over the soy sauce and cook for a few minutes, until glossy.

Season the steak with salt and pepper and cook on the barbecue grill until done to your liking. Set aside to rest, then slice.

**TO SERVE:** Spread each of the ciabatta roll bottoms with mayo and top with rocket and steak slices. Add a squeeze of mustard, then pile the onion mixture on top. Add the tops and eat immediately.

dish.co.nz | DISH 85

# Crayfish with Miso and Spring Onion Butter

*If you're lucky enough to have a diver in the family who might bring back the odd cray, this butter makes for a super delicious topping to complement the rich crayfish flesh. Please see the Cook's note about how to treat the crayfish before cooking.*

**SERVES 2-4**

**BUTTER**
50 grams butter, very soft but not melted

1 tablespoon white or yellow miso paste

1 spring onion, finely chopped

1 teaspoon grated fresh ginger

finely grated zest 1 lime

1 clove garlic, crushed

**TO COOK AND SERVE**
1 live crayfish (ours was 1.1 kilograms)

sea salt and ground pepper

2 teaspoons toasted sesame seeds

1 spring onion, finely shredded

**BUTTER:** Combine all the ingredients in a bowl.

**TO COOK AND SERVE:** After the crayfish has been put to sleep (see Cook's note), use a large kitchen knife to split the crayfish in half lengthwise.

Season the flesh side and lightly brush with the miso butter.

Place flesh side down on a preheated barbecue grill and cook for 2-3 minutes. Turn over and spread with the remaining butter. Cook for another 5 minutes, or until tender and cooked through.

Transfer to a platter and top with the sesame seeds and spring onion.

**COOK'S NOTE:** Put the live crayfish in the freezer for at least 1 hour to put it to sleep, then use a sharp, heavy knife to cut through the head, between the eyes.

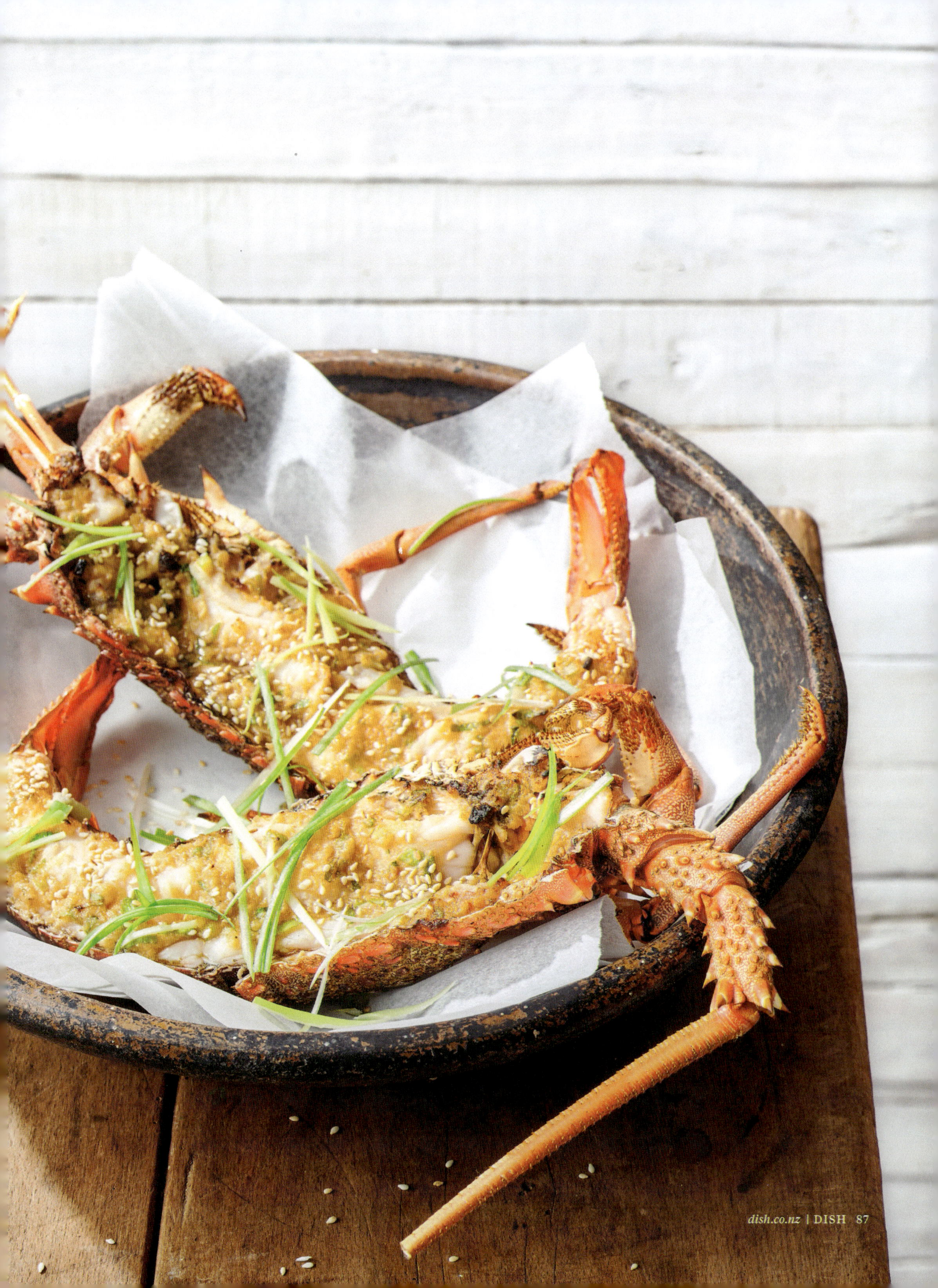

# Beer Can Chicken with White Barbecue Sauce

*A pretty hilarious way of cooking a chicken using a partially filled can of beer that is placed in the chicken's cavity prior to cooking. It results in juicy, tender meat with a deeply golden skin.*

**SERVES 6**

**SPICE RUB**
1 tablespoon brown sugar

1 teaspoon each ground cumin, smoked paprika, English mustard powder and sea salt

4 teaspoons olive oil

**TO COOK**
1.3-kilogram whole chicken

1 can beer

2 whole peeled cloves garlic, lightly smashed

1 sprig herbs, e.g., thyme or rosemary

**WHITE BARBECUE SAUCE**
¾ cup good-quality egg mayonnaise

2 tablespoons malt vinegar or apple cider vinegar

2 teaspoons each runny honey, Worcestershire sauce and Dijon mustard

1 tablespoon hot mustard

1 clove garlic, crushed

**SPICE RUB:** Combine all the ingredients in a small bowl.

**TO COOK:** Pat the chicken dry with kitchen towels. Rub the cavity with some of the spice rub, then spread the remaining rub all over the skin of the chicken.

Drink or pour out a third of the beer, then push the garlic and herbs into the can. Lower the chicken onto the can so it's sitting upright with the can in the cavity. Place in a shallow heatproof dish and pour in enough water to cover the base of the dish. Place the dish on the barbecue and lower the lid. Cook over a medium heat for about 1¼ hours, or until fully cooked, periodically adding more water to the dish so it doesn't dry out.

When the chicken is cooked, remove from the heat. Leave the chicken to rest for 10 minutes, then carefully remove from the can.

**WHITE BARBECUE SAUCE:** Whisk everything together in bowl until smooth.

**TO SERVE:** Cut the chicken into pieces and serve with the White Barbecue Sauce.

dish.co.nz | DISH 89

# Beef Short Ribs

*These meltingly tender, full-flavoured beef ribs are the stars on our barbecue. The ribs first need to be slow-cooked in the oven, then doused in tangy barbecue sauce and finished on the grill to transform them into sticky, smoky deliciousness. You can start this two days ahead.*

**MAKES 6 RIBS**

**RUB**
2 teaspoons sea salt

1 tablespoon brown sugar

1 teaspoon each ground cumin and paprika

½ teaspoon each ground coriander and chilli

**RIBS**
1.5 kilograms beef short ribs, or 6 ribs (see Cook's note)

2 tablespoons red wine vinegar

**GLAZE**
2 tablespoons American mustard

2 tablespoons tomato paste

2 tablespoons apple cider vinegar

2 tablespoons Worcestershire sauce

2 tablespoons melted butter

⅓ cup brown sugar

2 cloves garlic, crushed

¼–½ teaspoon chilli powder, to taste

½ teaspoon sea salt

Preheat the oven to 150°C regular bake.

**RUB:** Put all the ingredients in a bowl and rub together with your fingertips to combine well.

**RIBS:** Cut the ribs into single pieces and place bone side down in a baking dish. Sprinkle the rub over the meat, then rub onto all sides. Drizzle the vinegar over the top.

Cover tightly with foil and bake for 2½–3 hours, or until the meat is very tender. *Take care when handling the ribs as the meat will have shrunk away from the bone and can easily fall off while hot.*

Cool the ribs in the dish. *If cooking ahead, cover and refrigerate the ribs. Remove from the fridge 2 hours before grilling.*

**GLAZE:** Combine all the ingredients in a saucepan and bring to the boil. Simmer for 2 minutes, then transfer to a bowl. *This can be done ahead of time, just rewarm before using.*

**TO COOK:** Preheat the barbecue to low.

Scrape the fat off the ribs and brush the meat with a thin layer of glaze. Place on the bars of the grill and cook, turning and glazing every 5 minutes, until the meat is hot all the way through. *Don't let the glaze catch and burn.*

Place on a serving platter and serve topped with remaining glaze, with American mustard and crusty bread.

**COOK'S NOTE:** I buy the ribs according to how many I'm allowing for each person rather than by weight.

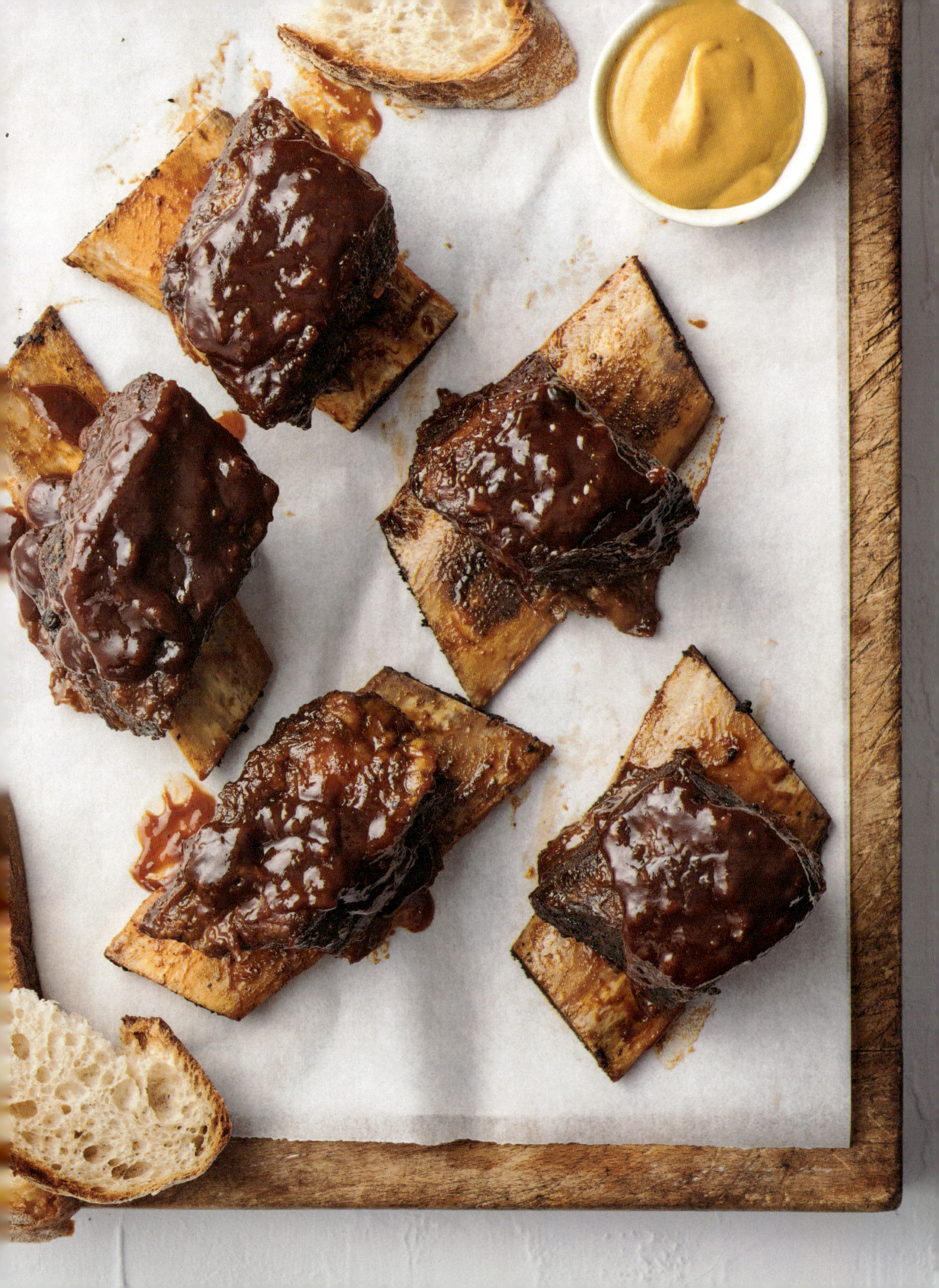

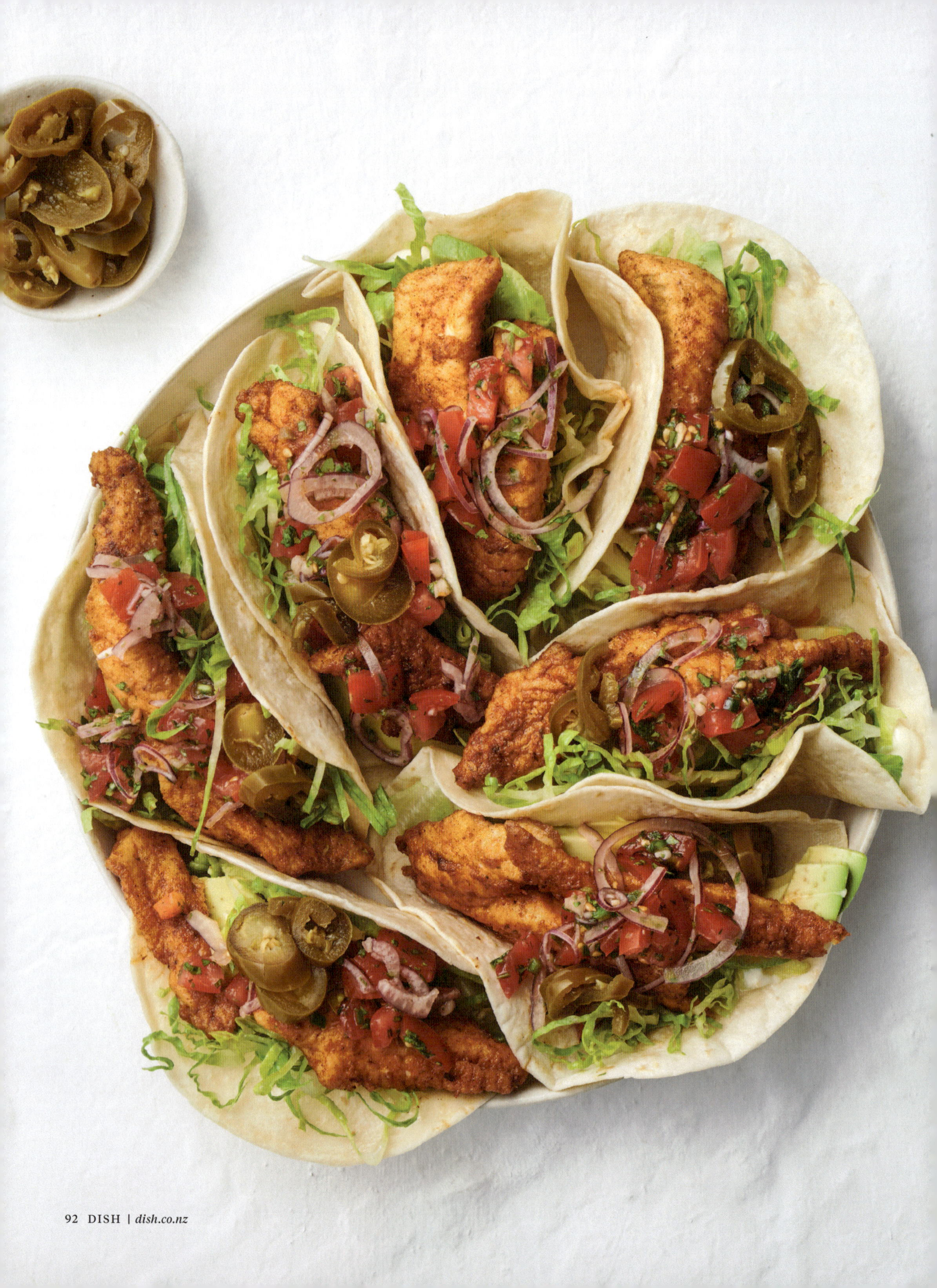

# Fish Tacos with Pico de Gallo

*Tender, spice-coated fish, a zesty salsa and creamy avocado are wrapped up in soft, warm tortillas for the perfect summer platter.*

**MAKES 8**

**FISH**

500 grams firm white fish

½ cup plain flour

2 tablespoons purchased Mexican spice mix

sea salt and ground pepper

olive oil

**PICO DE GALLO**

2 large, ripe tomatoes, roughly chopped

1 small red onion, thinly sliced

1 green chilli, finely chopped

2 cloves garlic, crushed

small handful coriander, finely chopped

2 tablespoons lime juice

1 tablespoon olive oil

**TO ASSEMBLE**

8 medium soft tortillas, warmed

good-quality egg mayonnaise

1 iceberg lettuce, shredded

2 avocados, sliced

½ cup sliced jalapeños in brine, drained

Cut the fish into 5cm pieces. Combine the flour and spice mix in a shallow bowl and season with salt and pepper. Toss through the fish to coat well.

Heat a little olive oil on a barbecue hot plate over a medium heat and fry the fish until just cooked.

**PICO DE GALLO:** Combine all the ingredients in a bowl and season.

**TO ASSEMBLE:** Spread each tortilla with mayonnaise, then fill with lettuce, avocado and fish. Spoon over the Pico de Gallo and top with jalapeños, serving the rest separately.

# Aromatic Peppercorn Chicken with Hot and Sweet Dipping Sauce (gf)

*These juicy, fragrant and intensely flavoured drumsticks are an easy option for popping on the barbecue. Don't leave out the dipping sauce – its sweet, sour and hot combo adds another layer of deliciousness.*

**SERVES 4**

**CHICKEN**
2 teaspoons each whole black peppercorns, cumin seeds and coriander seeds

1 teaspoon ground turmeric

½ cup chopped coriander roots and stems, plus 1 tablespoon finely chopped leaves, reserved to serve

6 cloves garlic, chopped

2 tablespoons grated fresh ginger

2 tablespoons fish sauce

1 teaspoon sea salt

2 tablespoons grapeseed oil

12 chicken drumsticks

**DIPPING SAUCE**
1 cup cider vinegar

1 cup caster sugar

4 cloves garlic, crushed

1½ teaspoons chilli flakes

1 teaspoon sea salt

**CUCUMBER SALAD**
1 telegraph cucumber

2 tablespoons rice vinegar

1 tablespoon sugar

1 teaspoon sea salt

⅓ cup roasted peanuts, roughly chopped

**CHICKEN:** Toast and grind all the whole spices. Blitz all the ingredients except the chicken in a food processor to make a thick paste. Scrape into a large bowl.

Slash the chicken a couple of times through the thickest part of the drumstick. Toss in the paste, pressing it into the slashes. Marinate in the fridge for 2-24 hours.

**DIPPING SAUCE:** Place the vinegar and sugar in a small saucepan and bring to the boil, stirring to dissolve the sugar. Simmer for 5 minutes, then take off the heat and stir in the garlic, chilli and salt. Cool and store in the fridge for up to 5 days.

**CUCUMBER SALAD:** Cut the cucumber in half lengthways and scrape out the seeds. Cut into 5cm lengths, then cut each piece into batons. Combine the vinegar, sugar and salt in a large bowl, add the cucumber and mix well. Toss through the peanuts just before serving.

**TO COOK AND SERVE:** Place the chicken on a barbecue flat plate over a medium heat. Cover and cook for about 25 minutes, or until the juices run clear.

Place on a platter and scatter over the reserved coriander leaves. Serve with the Dipping Sauce and the Cucumber Salad.

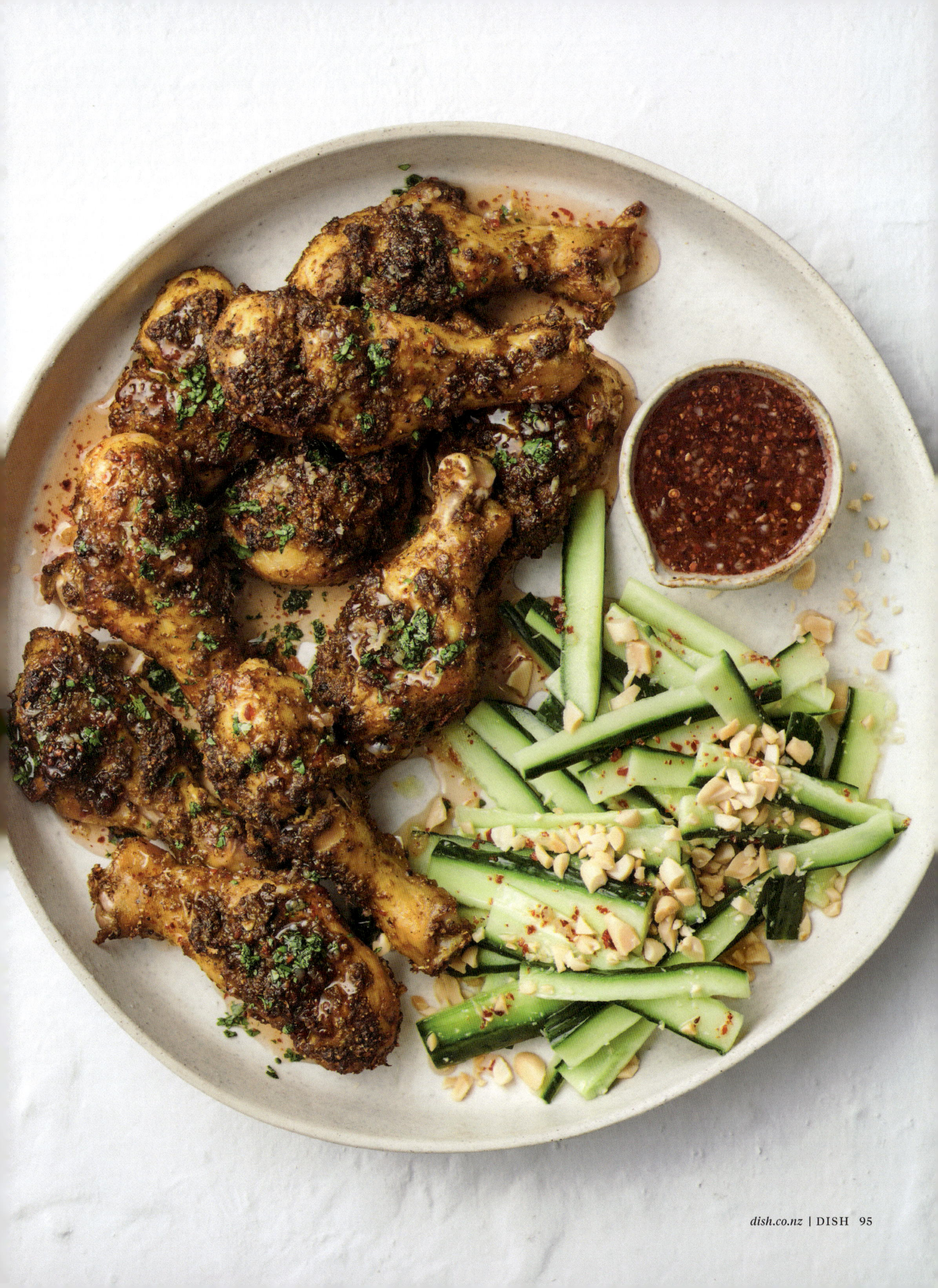

# Barbecued Butterflied Leg of Lamb with Herb and Parmesan Dressing (gf)

*Paired with a fresh herby dressing, this succulent butterflied leg of lamb will become a go-to when firing up the barbecue over summer.*

**SERVES 8**

**LAMB**

1.5-kilogram butterflied leg of lamb

sea salt and ground pepper

2 teaspoons cumin seeds

**DRESSING**

⅓ cup olive oil

¼ cup freshly grated parmesan

2 tablespoons lemon juice

¼ packed cup each basil and mint

1 tablespoon capers

2 cloves garlic, crushed

2 teaspoons honey

**TO SERVE**

1 cup thick plain yoghurt

2 handfuls watercress or rocket

**LAMB:** Season the lamb generously on both sides with salt and pepper and sprinkle over the cumin seeds.

Place skin side down on a barbecue preheated to medium and cook for about 12 minutes each side, or until cooked to your liking. Transfer to a plate, cover loosely and rest for 10 minutes.

**DRESSING:** Place all the ingredients in a food processor, season with salt and pepper and blitz until smooth.

**TO SERVE:** Spoon the yoghurt onto a large platter, then scatter over the watercress or rocket. Slice the lamb across the grain and arrange on top. Drizzle over any resting juices and spoon over some of the dressing, serving the rest separately.

dish.co.nz | DISH 97

# Chicken with Yoghurt, Caramelised Onions and Cashew Nuts (gf)

*Marinated chicken served with yoghurt, cashew nuts and caramelised onions is a fail-safe barbecue recipe.*

**SERVES 4**

**MARINADE**

½ cup thick plain yoghurt

finely grated zest and juice 1 lemon

3 cloves garlic, crushed

2 tablespoons grated fresh ginger

1 teaspoon sea salt

1 teaspoon each ground cinnamon and cardamom

½ teaspoon ground turmeric

6 bone-in, skin-on chicken thighs

**TOPPING**

3 tablespoons vegetable oil

knob of butter

3 red onions, thinly sliced

½ teaspoon sea salt

½ cup roughly chopped cashew nuts

½ cup white sultanas

**TO SERVE**

2 tablespoons purchased mango chutney

1 cup plain yoghurt

fresh coriander, to garnish

**MARINADE:** Whisk all the ingredients except the chicken together.

Put the chicken in a wide, shallow dish or large zip-lock bag and pour over the marinade, turning to coat. Cover and refrigerate for 2-24 hours.

**TOPPING:** Heat the oil and butter in a frying pan and add the onions and salt. Cover and cook for 10 minutes. Uncover and continue cooking gently until the onions are caramelised. *This will take at least 30 minutes.* Stir in the cashews and sultanas. *The topping can be made 2 days ahead, just reheat before serving.*

**TO COOK:** Preheat a barbecue hot plate to medium-low.

Remove the chicken from the marinade. Season and place on the barbecue. Cook for about 40 minutes, or until fully cooked.

**TO SERVE:** Fold the chutney through the yoghurt and spread over a platter. Arrange the chicken on top and spoon over the onions. Garnish with coriander.

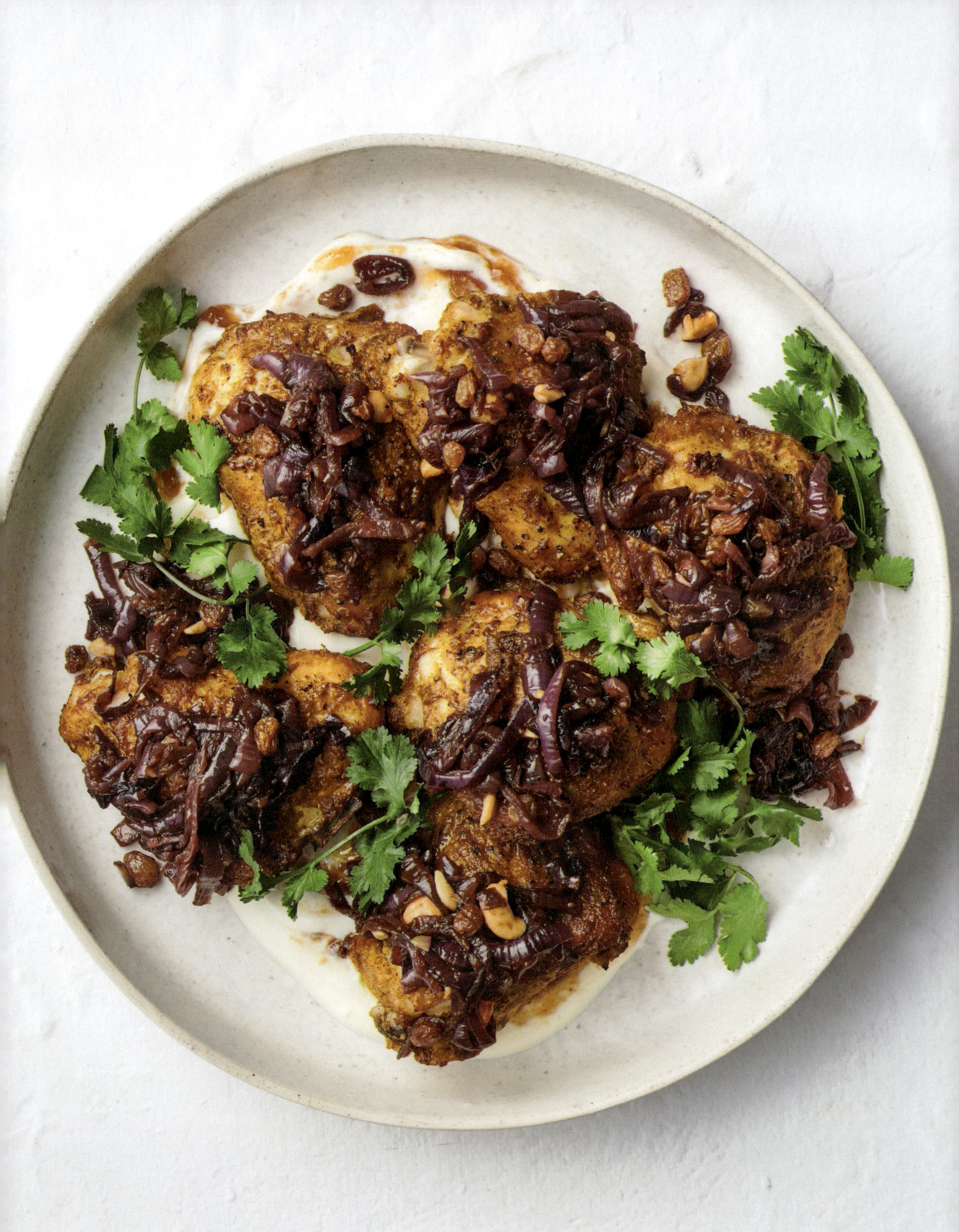

# BRING A SALAD

*That's the catch cry of almost every Kiwi host(ess) when asked what guests can bring to a summertime dinner – and invariably the offerings are all very similar... until now! Check out the Eggplant, Spinach and Couscous Salad with Lemony Yoghurt Dressing (page 118) and Warm Roasted Potato Salad with Parmesan, Walnut and Garlic Mayo (page 124), which threaten to be the star of the show. Meanwhile, the Barbecued Pork, Mango and Herb Salad (page 112) is practically a meal on its own. Next time the call goes out to 'bring a salad', let us help take your salad game to the next level.*

dish.co.nz | DISH 101

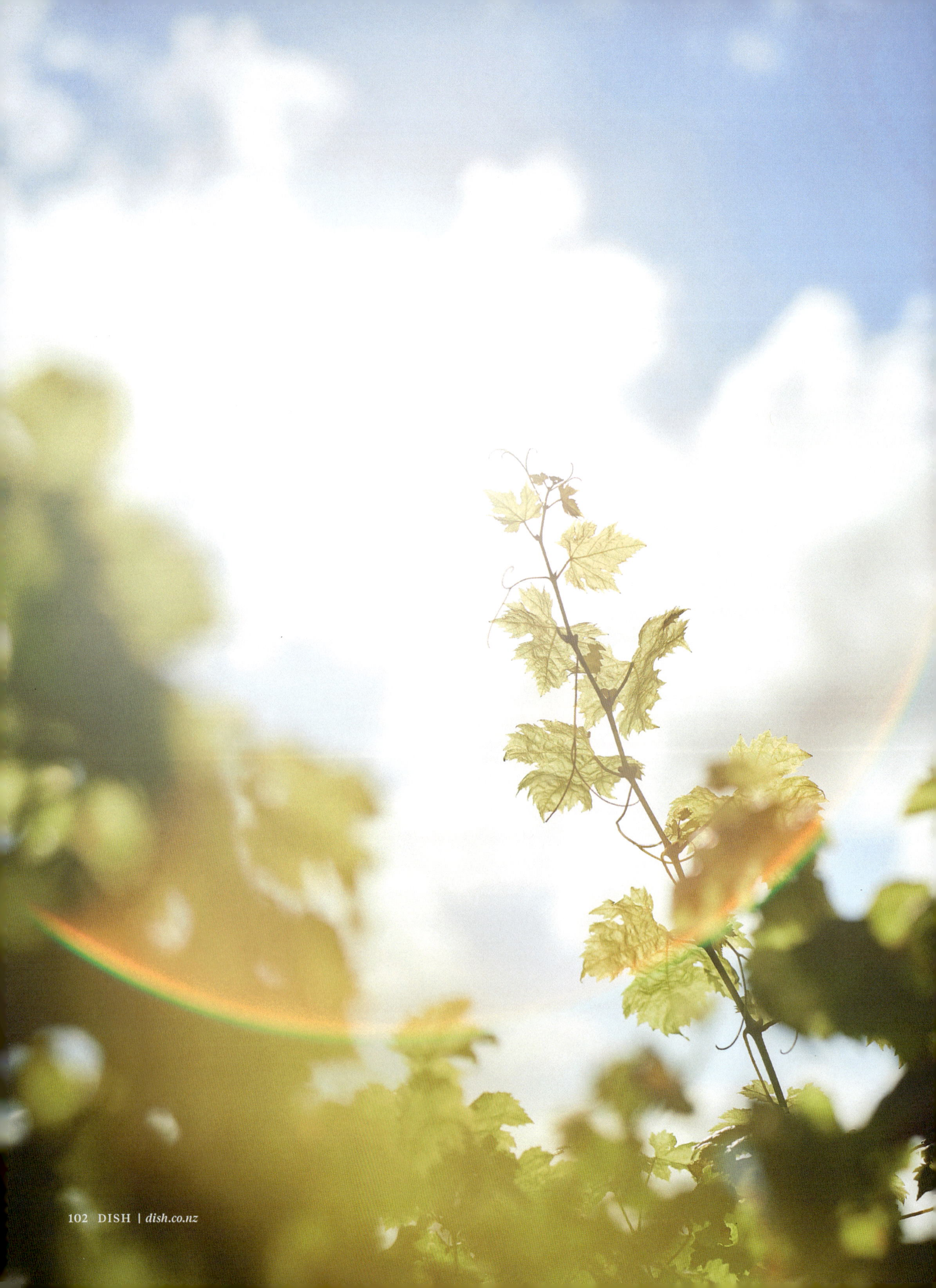

dish.co.nz | DISH 103

# Seeded Slaw (gf) (v)

*Toss the salad with the dressing just before serving so it retains a lovely crunchy texture and freshness.*

**SERVES 6**

**DRESSING**

¼ cup olive oil

1 teaspoon each finely grated orange zest and Dijon mustard

2 tablespoons orange juice

1 tablespoon sherry vinegar

2 cloves garlic, crushed

sea salt and ground pepper

**TO ASSEMBLE**

2 cups thinly sliced purple cabbage

2 cups thinly sliced green cabbage

1 small fennel bulb, thinly sliced, feathery tops reserved

1 cup julienned or finely shredded carrot

small handful parsley, finely chopped

¾ cup mixed seeds (I used a combination of toasted pumpkin, sunflower, sesame and poppy seeds)

**DRESSING:** Whisk all the ingredients together and season generously.

**TO ASSEMBLE:** Combine all the vegetables, parsley and three-quarters of the mixed seeds together in a large bowl. Roughly chop a small handful of the fennel tops and mix through.

Pour the dressing over the slaw and toss everything together to combine well.

Transfer to a serving bowl and top with the remaining seeds.

dish.co.nz | DISH 105

# Two-bean and Crisp Flatbread Salad with Soft Eggs (v)

*Shards of crisp bread, creamy white beans and a perky preserved lemon dressing make a light but substantial salad.*

**SERVES 4-6**

2 x 20cm Lebanese flatbreads

2 tablespoons melted butter

1 tablespoon olive oil

250 grams slim green beans, stem end trimmed

sea salt

**DRESSING**

1 tablespoon finely chopped preserved lemon skin, flesh discarded

4 tablespoons olive oil

1½ tablespoons lemon juice

2 cloves garlic, crushed

1 teaspoon runny honey

½ teaspoon sea salt

**TO SERVE**

2 handfuls watercress or rocket

400-gram tin cannellini beans, rinsed and drained

3 baby cucumbers or 1 small telegraph cucumber, thinly sliced

1 small red onion, very thinly sliced

4 boiled eggs, cut into quarters

small handful basil leaves

Preheat the oven to 180°C fan bake.

Brush both sides of the bread with butter and place on a flat baking tray. Bake for about 10 minutes, turning once, until golden and crisp. *The baked bread will stay crisp for 2-3 days in an airtight container.*

Heat the oil in a large frying pan and, when hot, add the beans. Cook for about 4 minutes, turning often, until lightly blistered in patches. Season with salt and set aside to cool.

**DRESSING:** Combine all the ingredients in a small bowl.

**TO SERVE:** Break the crisp flatbreads into large pieces. Layer up the watercress, green and white beans, cucumber, onion, eggs and basil on a large platter, tucking in some of the bread. Drizzle over the dressing. Serve the remaining bread separately.

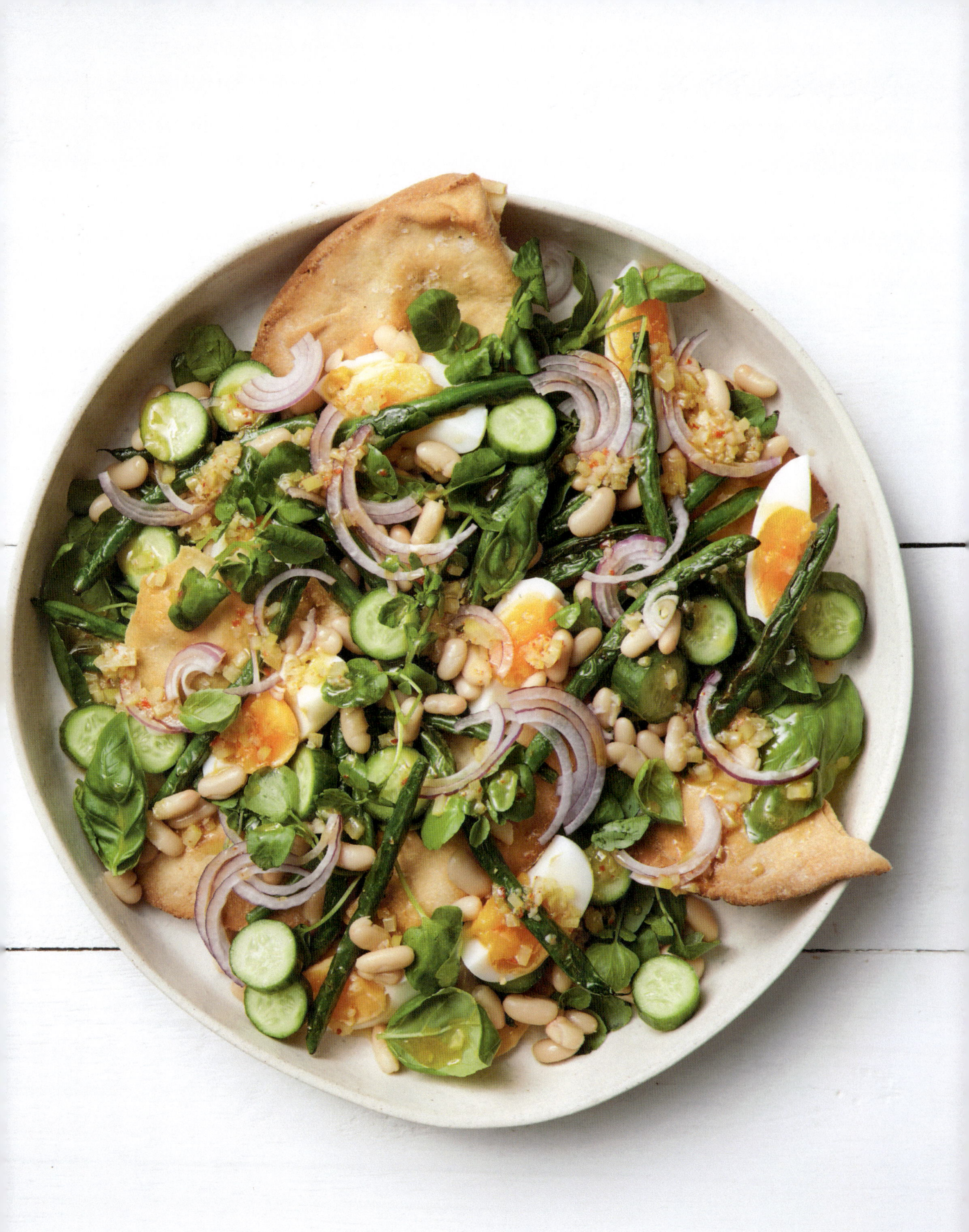

# Knock-your-socks-off Croutons, Fresh Tomato, Prosciutto and Mozzarella Salad

*This is summer in a bowl and it's all about fantastic tomatoes and basil, tender prosciutto and big, garlicky, cheesy croutons.*

**SERVES 4**

**CROUTONS**
1 loaf sourdough bread, all the crust cut off

½ cup olive oil

3 cloves garlic, crushed

1½ cups freshly grated parmesan

sea salt and ground pepper

**DRESSING**
3 tablespoons each basil pesto and olive oil

2 tablespoons lemon juice

**TO SERVE**
800 grams mixed tomatoes, cut however you want

2 tablespoons olive oil

8 thin slices prosciutto

2 x 125-gram balls fresh mozzarella in whey, drained and ripped into pieces

1 cup basil leaves

1 cup pitted green olives

Preheat the oven to 180°C fan bake.

**CROUTONS:** Rip the bread into large bite-sized pieces and place in a large bowl. Whisk the oil and garlic together, then pour over the bread. Scrunch together with your hands, then sprinkle over the parmesan and season generously with salt and pepper. Scrunch again, then tip onto a baking tray, scraping over any oil or cheese left in the bowl. Spread evenly and bake for about 20 minutes, turning the pieces halfway through cooking, until golden and crisp on the outside and tender in the centre. Set aside (and try not to eat them all).

**DRESSING:** Whisk all the ingredients together in a bowl and season with salt and pepper.

**TO SERVE:** Toss the tomatoes with the oil and season generously with salt and pepper. Place on a platter and top with the prosciutto, croutons, ripped mozzarella, basil and olives. Drizzle everything with the dressing.

dish.co.nz | DISH 109

110  DISH | dish.co.nz

# Lemony Sumac Chicken and Chickpea Salad with Dates, Feta and Baby Spinach

*This salad is on high rotation over summer and I encourage friends to scoop up the salad with the crisp flatbreads.*

**SERVES 4-6**

6 skinless, boneless chicken thighs

sea salt and ground pepper

2 tablespoons sumac

3 tablespoons olive oil

400-gram tin chickpeas, rinsed and drained

2 tablespoons lemon juice

2 tablespoons butter

2 medium pita flatbreads, ripped into large pieces

**TO ASSEMBLE**
2 cups baby spinach leaves

1 small telegraph cucumber, sliced

½ cup parsley leaves

1 red onion, very thinly sliced, tossed with 2 tablespoons lemon juice

6 fresh dates, pitted, quartered lengthways

150 grams soft marinated feta

½ cup pomegranate arils

citrus olive oil, for drizzling over

Season the chicken and sprinkle with the sumac. Heat 1 tablespoon of the oil in a frying pan over a medium heat.

Cook the chicken for 8 minutes, or until cooked through. Transfer to a plate, cover loosely and rest for a few minutes. *Don't wash the pan.*

Add the chickpeas to the pan and cook until golden, stirring frequently. *Take care as they can spit.* Stir in the lemon juice and let it bubble up, then scrape into a bowl. Wash the pan and add 1 tablespoon each of butter and oil. Cook the bread in batches until deeply golden in patches and crisp. Place on kitchen towels and sprinkle with salt. Add the remaining butter and oil to the pan as needed between batches.

**TO ASSEMBLE:** Slice the chicken. Layer up the spinach, chickpeas, cucumber and parsley on a platter. Top with the chicken, drained red onions, dates, spoonfuls of the feta and pomegranate arils. Spoon over the chicken resting juices and a generous drizzle of the citrus olive oil.

# Barbecued Pork, Mango and Herb Salad

*This spice marinade is also delicious on chicken and prawns.*

**SERVES 4-6**

2 teaspoons each ground coriander and ground fennel

1 teaspoon each ground turmeric and ground cumin

2 cloves garlic, crushed

1 tablespoon grated fresh ginger

½ teaspoon ground chilli

2 tablespoons vegetable oil

4 pork scotch steaks

sea salt

**DRESSING**

3 tablespoons each fish sauce and lime juice

1 tablespoon brown sugar

1 long red chilli, finely chopped

2 cloves garlic, crushed

**TO SERVE**

1 large mango, peeled, sliced

1 cup bean sprouts

2 spring onions, thinly sliced

1 small telegraph cucumber, halved, seeded, sliced

½ cup each mint, coriander, and Thai basil leaves

40 grams crispy pork crackling, roughly chopped (optional, see Cook's note)

Mix the spices, garlic, ginger, chilli and oil together, then rub over the pork. Cover and chill for 1-24 hours. Season the pork with sea salt and cook on a preheated barbecue or in a little oil in a large frying pan over a medium-high heat. Cook for 3 minutes each side, or until just cooked through. Transfer to a plate and rest for 5 minutes.

**DRESSING:** Stir all the ingredients together to dissolve the sugar.

**TO SERVE:** Arrange half the mango, bean sprouts, spring onions, cucumber and herbs on a large platter. Top with the sliced pork, then the remaining salad ingredients. Spoon the dressing over everything, then top with the pork crackling, if using.

**COOK'S NOTE:** Cooked pork crackling is available at specialty food stores and Asian supermarkets.

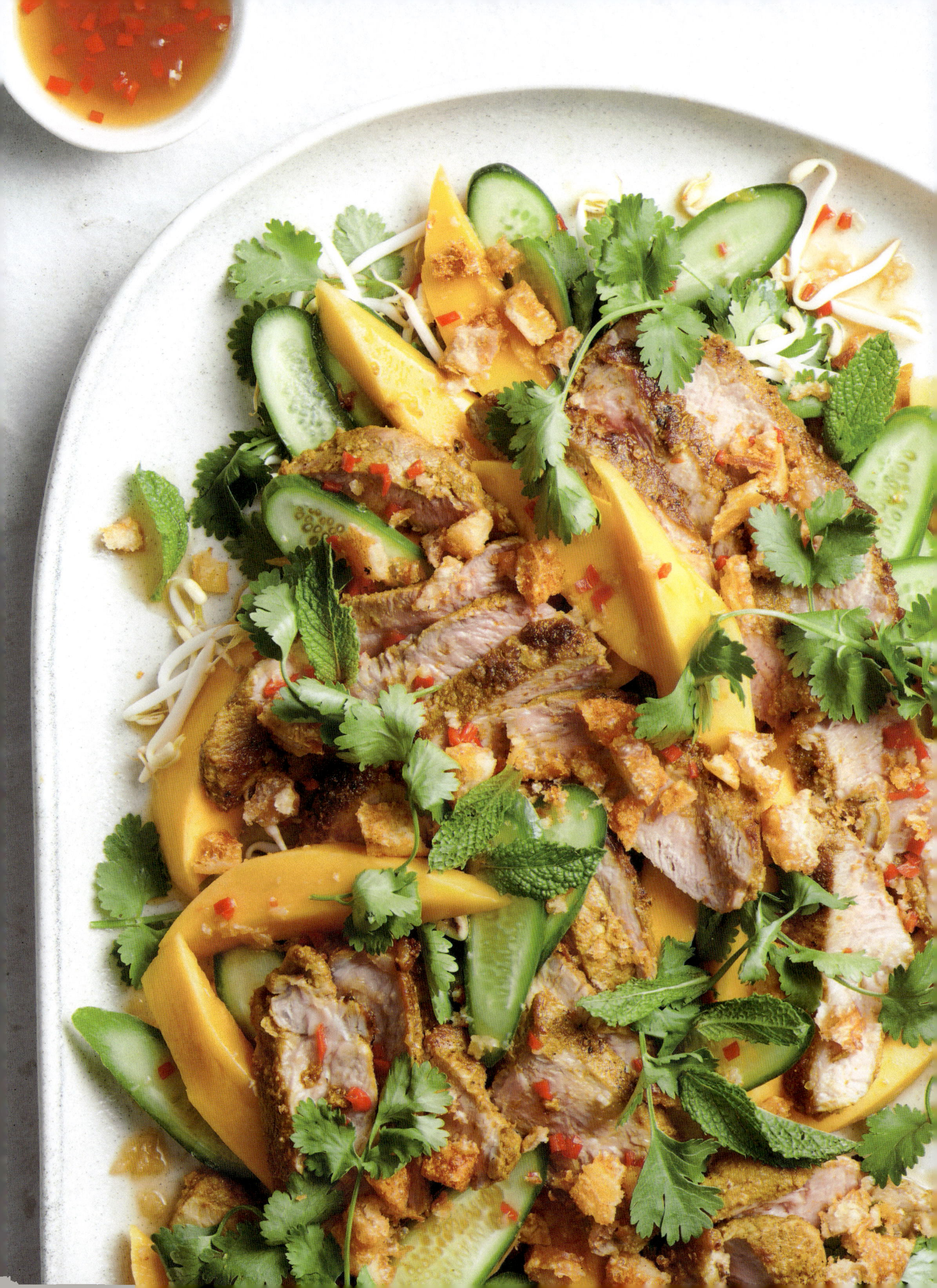

# Roasted Veg and Udon Noodle Salad (v)

*A versatile and speedy salad, this flavoursome noodle dish is a tasty addition to any summer barbie.*

**SERVES 4-6**

3 medium orange kūmara, peeled and roughly chopped into 3-4cm chunks

1 red capsicum, roughly chopped

2 red onions, halved and cut into wedges through the root

2 tablespoons olive oil

1 tablespoon sesame oil

2 tablespoons sweet chilli sauce

1 tablespoon honey

1 tablespoon soy sauce

300 grams udon noodles

**DRESSING**
1 tablespoon each olive oil and sesame oil

1 tablespoon soy sauce

1 tablespoon rice wine vinegar

**TO SERVE**
1 cup edamame beans, cooked

½ cup chopped roasted cashews, 2 tablespoons reserved to garnish

¼ cup coriander, finely chopped

1 tablespoon black or white sesame seeds, toasted

**EQUIPMENT:** Line a large roasting dish with baking paper.

Preheat the oven to 180°C fan bake.

Put the kūmara, capsicum and onion in the lined roasting dish. Whisk both the oils, sweet chilli sauce, honey and soy sauce together and drizzle over the vegetables. Bake for about 25 minutes, or until cooked through, turning once during cooking. Set aside to cool.

Cook the noodles according to the packet instructions. Drain and rinse under cold water. Drain again and place in a large bowl.

**DRESSING:** Whisk all the ingredients together in a small bowl.

**TO SERVE:** Add the roasted vegetables, edamame beans, cashews and coriander to the noodles. Add the dressing and toss gently to combine.

Transfer to a serving bowl and sprinkle with the reserved cashews and sesame seeds.

dish.co.nz | DISH 115

# Spice-roasted Carrot and Avocado Salad (gf) (v)

*Roasted carrots shine in this salad, thanks to the combination of rich avocado, crunchy dukkah and a smoky vinaigrette.*

**SERVES 4-6**

8 medium carrots, peeled and halved lengthways

2 teaspoons each cumin seeds and fennel seeds, toasted and roughly ground

2 tablespoons maple syrup or honey

2 tablespoons olive oil

sea salt and ground pepper

**DRESSING**

3 tablespoons olive oil

1 tablespoon sherry or red wine vinegar

1 clove garlic, crushed

½ teaspoon smoked paprika

1 teaspoon orange zest

2 tablespoons orange juice

**TO SERVE**

2 big handfuls salad leaves

2 avocados, peeled and sliced

180 grams stracciatella or mozzarella in whey, drained

2 tablespoons dukkah

⅓ cup pomegranate arils

¼ cup fresh dill

Preheat the oven to 180°C fan bake.

Place the carrots on a lined baking tray. Stir the seeds, maple syrup or honey and olive oil together in a small bowl, then pour over the carrots and toss together. Season with salt and pepper and spread into a single layer.

Roast for about 30 minutes, turning occasionally, until just tender and golden. Cool.

**DRESSING:** Whisk all the ingredients together in a bowl and season.

**TO SERVE:** Scatter the salad leaves over a large platter. Arrange the carrots and avocado on top, then tuck in the stracciatella. Spoon over the dressing and scatter with the dukkah, pomegranate arils and dill.

dish.co.nz | DISH 117

# Eggplant, Spinach and Couscous Salad with Lemony Yoghurt Dressing (v)

*Stracciatella or fresh mozzarella would be a delicious option in place of the burrata.*

**SERVES 4-6**

2 large eggplants, cut into 1½cm-thick rounds

olive oil, for brushing

sea salt and ground pepper

1 cup couscous

1 cup boiling water

¼ cup currants

1 teaspoon ground cumin

1 tablespoon olive oil

2 big handfuls baby spinach

**DRESSING**

1 cup thick plain yoghurt

2 tablespoons olive oil

finely grated zest 1 lemon

1 tablespoon lemon juice

1 tablespoon tahini

1 teaspoon Dijon mustard

2 cloves garlic, crushed

1 teaspoon sea salt

**TO SERVE**

125-gram ball fresh burrata in whey, drained

¼ cup pistachios, roughly chopped

¼ cup mint, thinly sliced

chilli flakes

Preheat the oven to 180°C fan bake.

Brush both sides of the eggplant with oil and season with salt and pepper. Place on a large, lined baking tray and roast for about 25 minutes, or until tender but not falling apart. Set aside.

Combine the couscous, water, currants, cumin and oil in a heatproof bowl with 1 teaspoon sea salt. Cover and set aside for 10 minutes, then fluff up with a fork. Add the spinach and toss together.

**DRESSING:** Blitz all the ingredients together in a food processor.

**TO SERVE:** Spread the dressing over a serving platter. Top with the couscous and eggplant, then break over the burrata. Scatter over the pistachios, mint and a good pinch of chilli flakes.

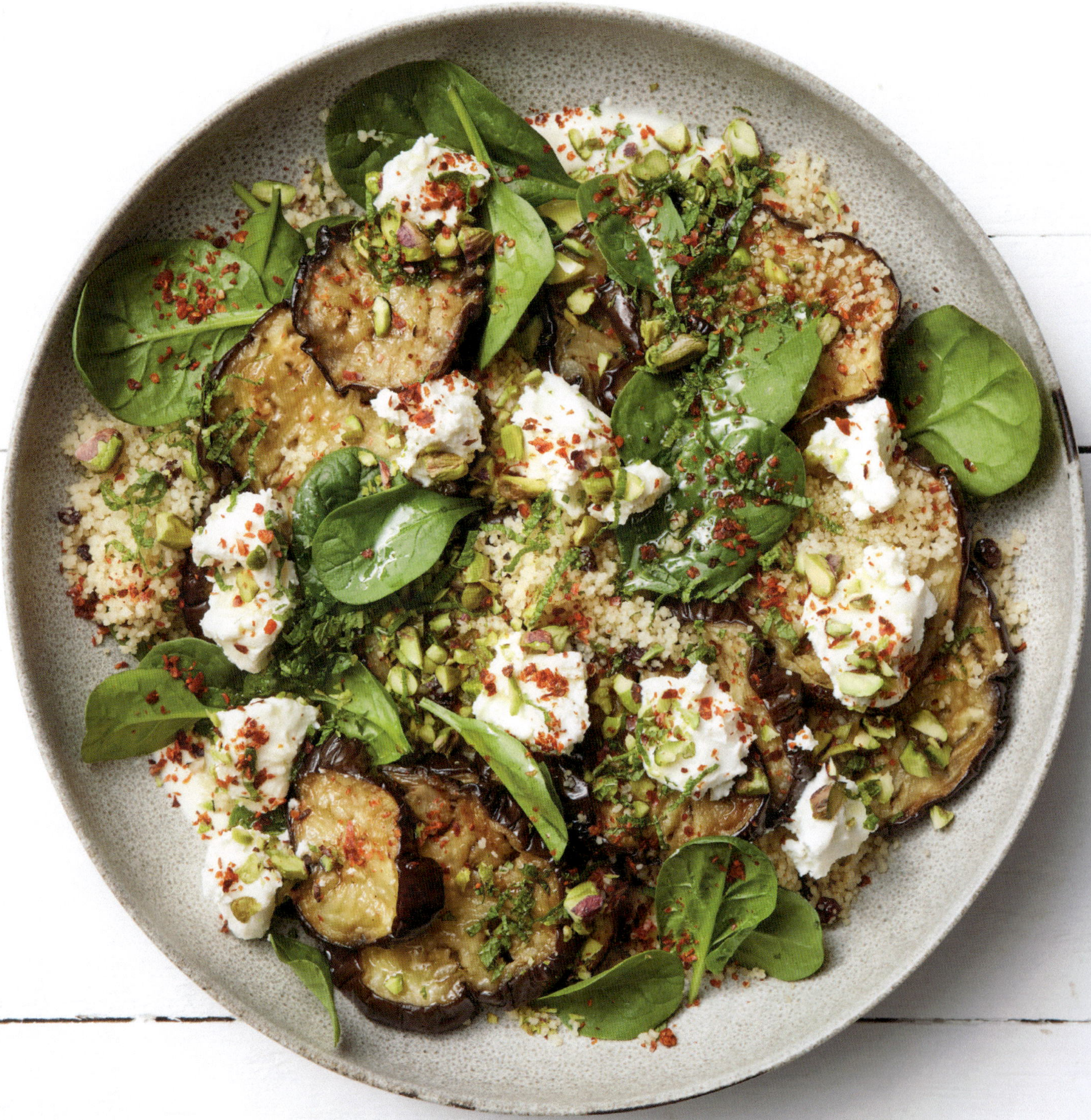

# Luscious Tomatoes, Baked Eggplant and Mozzarella Salad (gf) (v)

*Use the biggest, juiciest tomatoes you can find when making this salad. You could also substitute beautiful creamy strands of stracciatella for the mozzarella.*

**SERVES 6**

2 medium eggplants, sliced into 2cm-thick rounds

olive oil, for brushing

sea salt and ground pepper

**DRESSING**

3 tablespoons olive oil

1 tablespoon lemon juice

2 cloves garlic, crushed

1 teaspoon runny honey

**TO SERVE**

3 large heirloom tomatoes, sliced

2 x 125-gram balls fresh mozzarella in whey, well drained

basil leaves for garnish

Preheat the oven to 180°C fan bake.

Brush both sides of the eggplant slices with olive oil and season with salt and pepper. Place on a lined baking tray and roast for about 20 minutes, or until tender and golden. Set aside.

**DRESSING:** Whisk all the ingredients together and season with salt and pepper.

**TO SERVE:** Arrange the tomatoes and eggplant on a large serving platter. Rip over the mozzarella, then drizzle over the dressing. Scatter over the basil and season with salt and a grind of pepper.

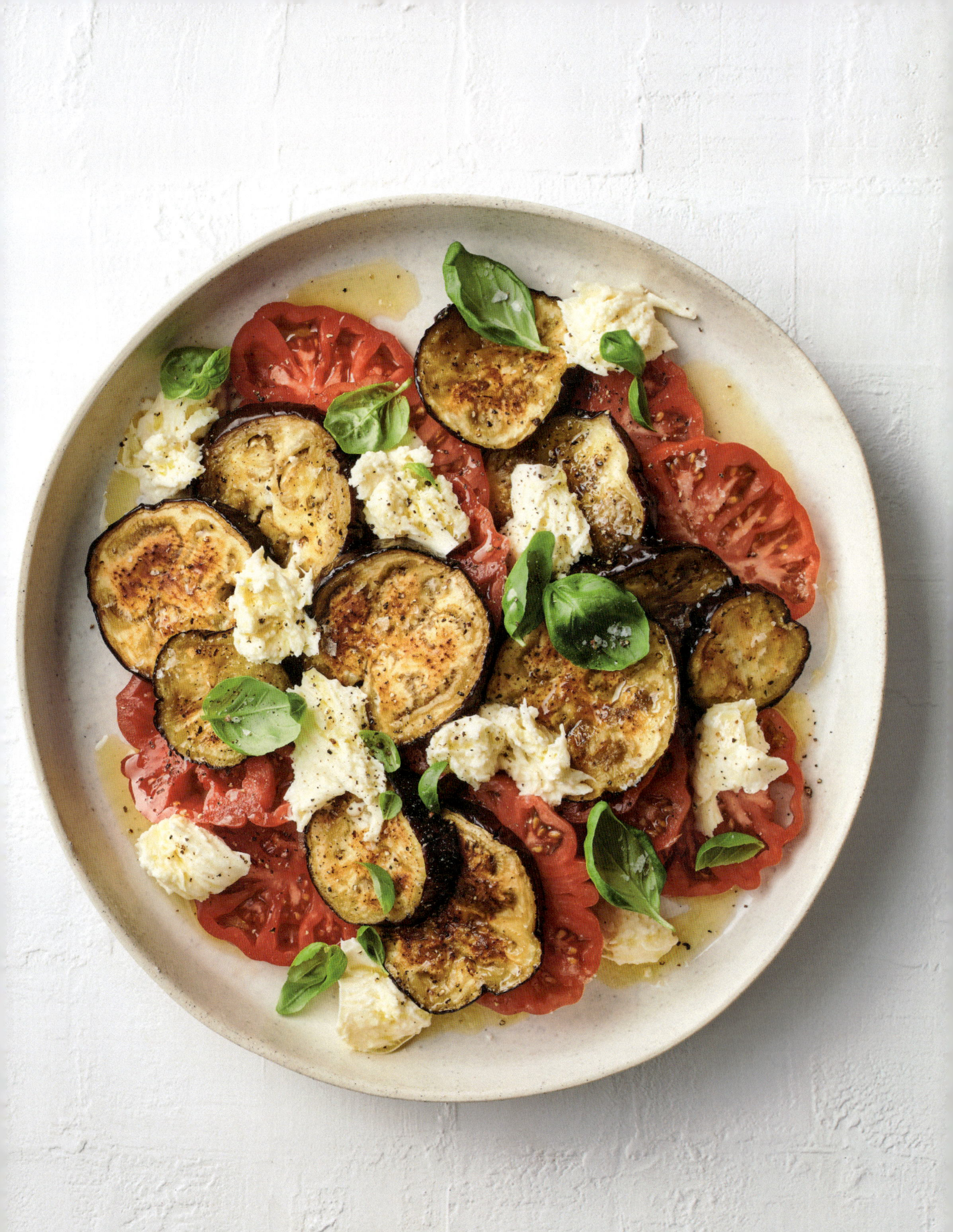

# Smoked Chicken and Mango Salad with Crispy Noodles and Peanut Dressing

*After making the dressing, this is a simple put-together, perfect for casual entertaining.*

**SERVES 4-6**

**DRESSING**
½ cup roasted peanuts

¼ cup sweet chilli sauce

2 cloves garlic, crushed

1 tablespoon soy sauce

1 tablespoon fish sauce

1 teaspoon sesame oil

finely grated zest 1 lime

2 tablespoons fresh lime juice

1 tablespoon each vegetable oil and water

**SALAD**
1 smoked double chicken breast

1 mango, peeled and sliced

2 spring onions, thinly sliced

½ cup sliced water chestnuts

1 cos lettuce, thinly sliced

1 avocado, peeled and sliced

2 cups crispy noodles

2 handfuls rocket

2 handful coriander

**DRESSING:** Put all the ingredients in a food processor and blitz until the peanuts are finely chopped.

**SALAD:** Remove the skin and any fat from the chicken and slice thinly. Layer with all the other ingredients on a large platter. Drizzle with some of the dressing, serving the rest separately.

dish.co.nz | DISH 123

# Warm Roasted Potato Salad with Parmesan, Walnut and Garlic Mayo (gf) (v)

*Transform hot roasted potatoes by tossing them through a garlicky, nutty mayonnaise and you have a delicious accompaniment to any meal.*

**SERVES 6-8**

800 grams waxy potatoes, scrubbed (we used assorted colours)

2 red onions, peeled with root left on

10 cloves garlic, skin on

3 tablespoons olive oil

sea salt and ground pepper

**DRESSING**

⅓ cup walnuts, toasted

½ cup good-quality egg mayonnaise

1 tablespoon olive oil

1 tablespoon wholegrain mustard

2 tablespoons freshly grated parmesan, plus extra for garnish

2-3 teaspoons lemon juice or white wine vinegar

2 tablespoons finely chopped parsley

Preheat the oven to 200°C regular bake.

Cut the potatoes into large chunks, leaving any tiny ones whole, and slice each onion into 6 wedges through the root end. Toss the potatoes, onions and garlic with the olive oil and place in a single layer on a large baking tray. Season generously.

Roast for about 40 minutes, until the potatoes are golden and tender, turning everything a couple of times and removing the onions and garlic when cooked. *The potatoes will take longer to cook.*

**DRESSING:** Squeeze the flesh from 6 of the roasted garlic cloves into a bowl. Add 2 tablespoons of the walnuts, finely chopped, and the mayonnaise, olive oil, mustard and parmesan. Add the lemon juice or vinegar to taste. Season with salt and pepper.

**TO SERVE:** Toss the remaining garlic cloves, warm potatoes and onions with enough dressing to coat and transfer to a serving bowl. Scatter with the remaining walnuts, extra parmesan, parsley and freshly ground pepper. Serve the remaining dressing separately.

*dish.co.nz* | DISH 125

# Roasted Beetroot, Blue Cheese and Pistachio Salad (gf) (v)

*Roasted beetroot are like glowing precious stones. Add a rich pomegranate dressing and creamy blue cheese for an impressive but easy entrée, light meal or side.*

**SERVES 6-8**

20 baby or 10 small beetroot, tops trimmed (I used gold and purple)

olive oil

sea salt and ground pepper

**DRESSING**

2 tablespoons pomegranate molasses

2 teaspoons red wine vinegar

2 teaspoons honey

2 teaspoons water

4 tablespoons olive oil

2 cloves garlic, crushed

**TO SERVE**

handful salad leaves

150 grams creamy blue cheese

2 tablespoons pistachios

Preheat the oven to 180°C fan bake.

Wash the beetroot, then place in a large piece of foil. *Put the different colours on separate pieces of foil.*

Drizzle with a little olive oil, salt and pepper. Seal tightly and place on a baking tray. Roast the beetroot for 50 minutes, or until tender.

When cool enough to handle, gently peel off the skins. *Disposable gloves are highly recommended for this.*

**DRESSING:** Whisk all the ingredients in a bowl and season.

**TO SERVE:** Arrange the salad leaves and beetroot on a serving platter. Drizzle with some of the dressing, then crumble over the blue cheese. Scatter with the pistachios and serve the remaining dressing separately.

*dish.co.nz* | DISH 127

# Mixed Tomato Salad with Tahini Yoghurt and Crisp Capers (gf) (v)

*Juicy, sweet tomatoes, creamy tahini and crisp salty capers make a simple but super tasty summer salad.*

**SERVES 6-8**

**TAHINI YOGHURT**
1 cup thick plain yoghurt

½ cup tahini

2 tablespoons cold water

finely grated zest 1 lemon

2 tablespoons lemon juice

2 cloves garlic, crushed

1½ teaspoons sea salt

**CRISP CAPERS**
3 tablespoons olive oil

½ cup capers, patted dry with kitchen towels

**TO SERVE**
800 grams assorted tomatoes, roughly chopped

zest 1 lemon

olive oil, for drizzling over

ground pepper

**TAHINI YOGHURT:** Whisk everything together in a bowl until smooth. Cover and refrigerate for 1 hour to firm up. *This can be made up to 2 days ahead of using.*

**CRISP CAPERS:** Heat the olive oil in a small frying pan and when moderately hot, add the capers and cook for about 4 minutes, stirring occasionally, until they have puffed up a little and are crisp. Drain on kitchen towels.

**TO SERVE:** Spoon the tahini yoghurt onto a lipped serving plate, then use the back of a spoon to push it out to make a thick edge around the outside. Spoon the tomatoes into the centre. Scatter over the lemon zest and capers, then drizzle everything with olive oil and a grinding of pepper.

*dish.co.nz* | DISH 129

# Crisp Lettuce and Asparagus Salad with Tarragon Aioli And Soft Eggs (gf)

*A fabulous combination of crisp lettuce, creamy aioli and tart olives, anchovies and capers.*

**SERVES 6-8**

**TARRAGON AIOLI**
½ cup good-quality egg mayonnaise

1½ teaspoons dried tarragon

2 cloves garlic, crushed

finely grated zest 1 lemon

3 teaspoons lemon juice

1 teaspoon Dijon mustard

sea salt and ground pepper

**SALAD**
2 cos lettuces

12-16 slim asparagus, blanched

4 large eggs, soft-boiled and halved

2 tablespoons capers

8 good-quality anchovies

12 black olives, pitted

parmesan, for shaving over

**AILOI:** Whisk all the ingredients together in a bowl and season.

**TO SERVE:** Cut the lettuces into wedges through the root and place on a serving platter along with the asparagus and eggs. Spoon over some of the aioli and scatter over the capers, anchovies and olives. Shave over some parmesan and serve the remaining aioli separately.

*dish*.co.nz | DISH 131

# Avocado, Broad Bean and Goat's Cheese Salad (gf) (v)

*I've seen a few iterations of salad with these components, but the thing I love about this version is the addition of both salty feta and milky mozzarella to contrast with the peppery watercress, fresh herbs and sweet peas and beans. The final touch is a sprinkling of chilli and dukkah for heat and texture. Perfect with the Roast Salmon on page 58.*

**SERVES 8**

2 cups broad beans

1 cup frozen peas

few sprigs mint

2 tablespoons olive oil

¼ cup lemon juice

1 teaspoon caster sugar

sea salt and ground pepper

6 cups baby watercress or other salad greens

2 large avocados, sliced

350 grams buffalo mozzarella, torn into chunks

200 grams feta, crumbled

¾ cup fresh mint leaves

2 tablespoons roughly chopped dill

chilli flakes and purchased dukkah, for sprinkling over

Bring a medium pot of water to the boil and fill a bowl with cold water and a few ice cubes. Drop the broad beans into the boiling water and cook just until the water comes back up to the boil. Remove the beans with a slotted spoon and put them straight into the chilled water. Drop the peas into the same boiling water for 1 minute, then drain and refresh under cold running water.

Gently pop the beans from their pods and add to the peas along with a few sprigs of mint (remove before serving) and refrigerate both in a covered container, if preparing ahead.

Whisk together the olive oil, lemon juice, sugar, salt and pepper.

**TO SERVE:** Layer the watercress onto a platter, followed by the avocado, mozzarella, beans and peas, feta, mint leaves and dill. Drizzle with the lemon dressing and sprinkle with chilli flakes and dukkah.

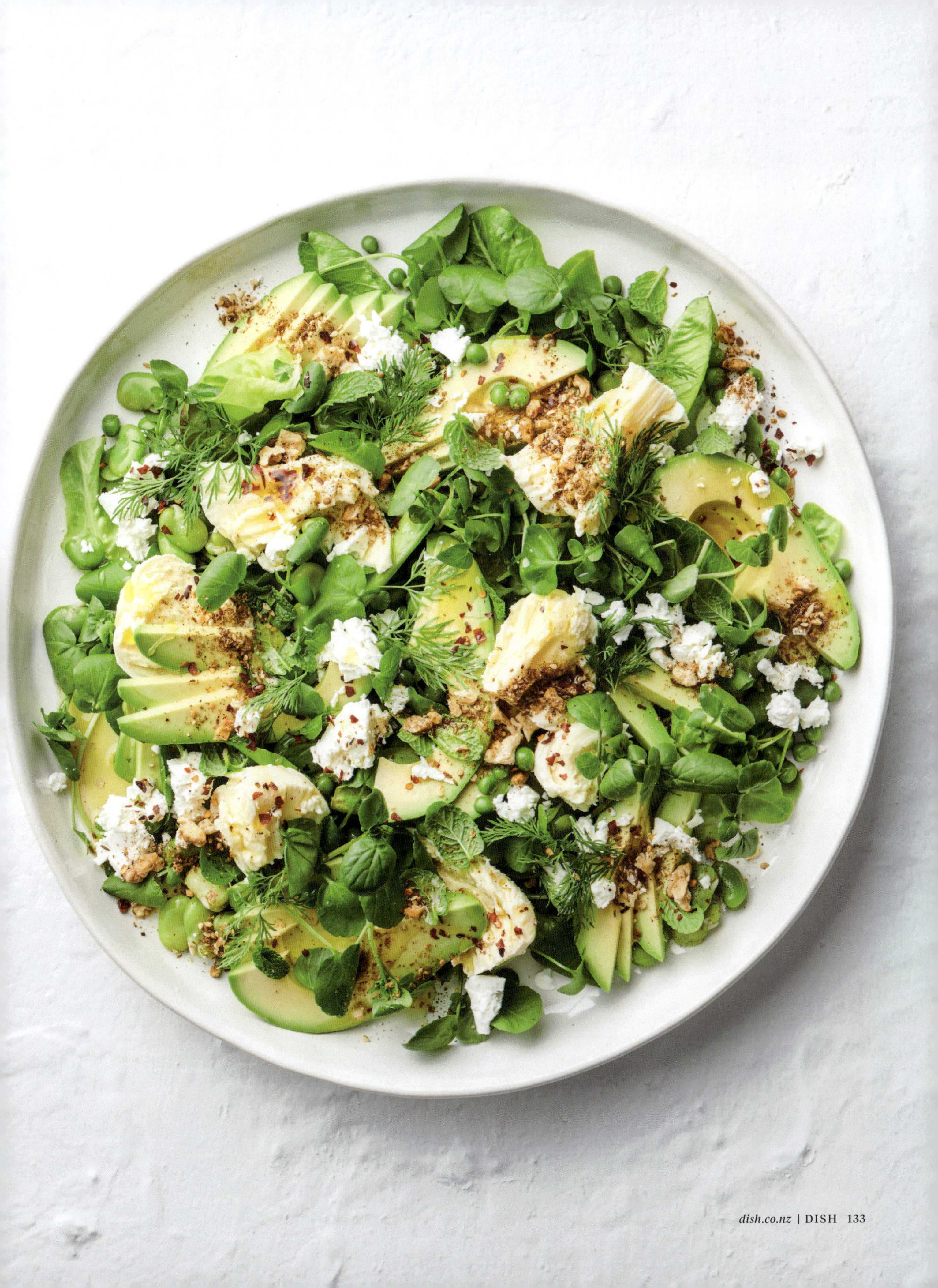

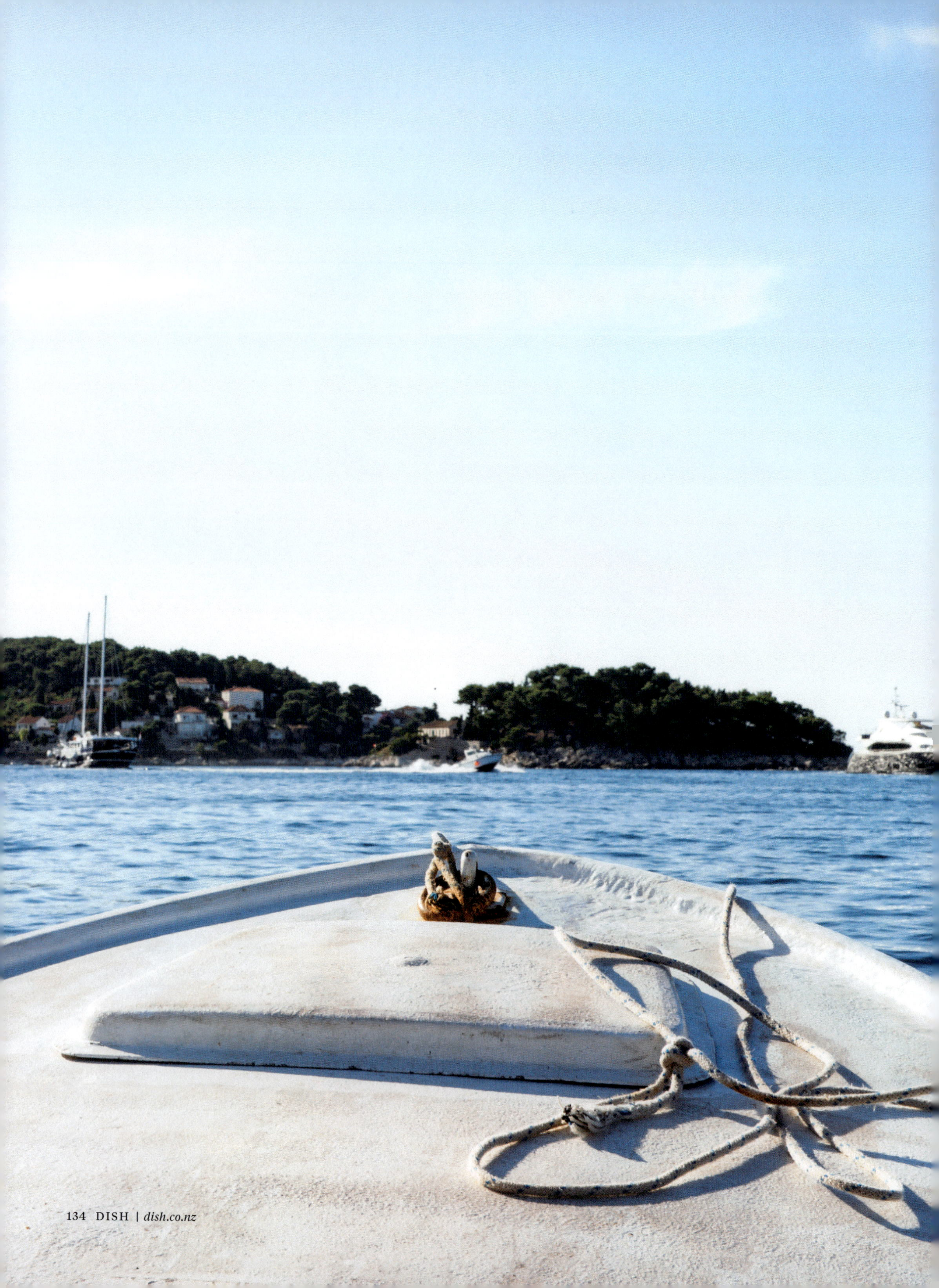

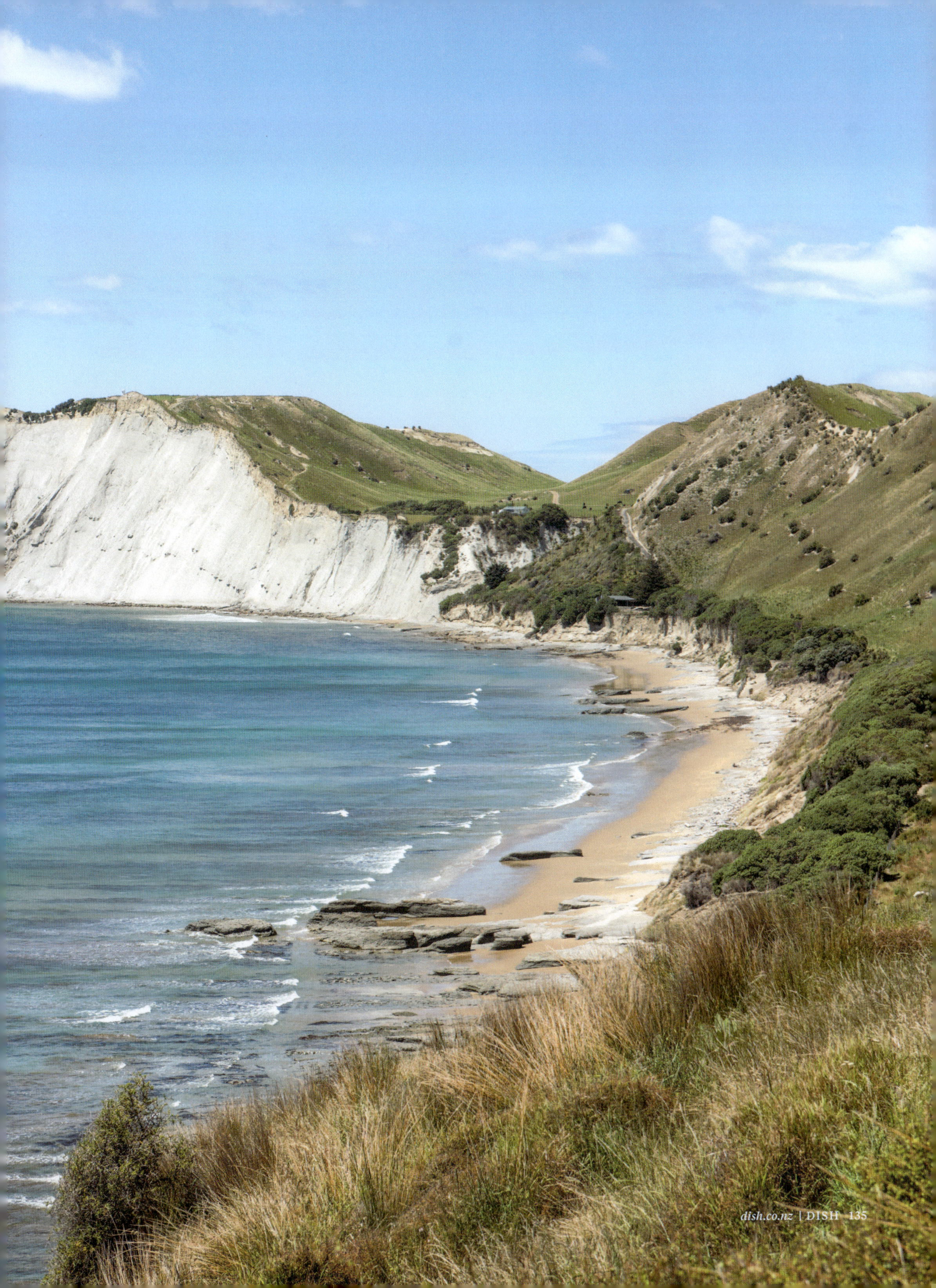

# BURGER MANIA

*One of life's simplest pleasures is taking a big bite out of a loaded burger as you break through soft bun to the layered goodies inside – there is something so deeply satisfying about getting so many flavours and textures in one mouthful! Here we present the all-time favourite Kiwi Lamb Burger (page 138), appropriately crammed with beetroot, tomato and a soft-fried egg, before taking a walk on the wild side with Crispy Spiced Onion Fritter Burgers with Mango Chutney (page 140), Chorizo and Garlic Prawn Burgers (page 144) and the vibrant Moroccan Lamb Burgers with Grilled Haloumi and Pistachio Salsa (page 146). With so many options, we reckon the only solution is to work your way through the whole section... before you start again!*

dish.co.nz | DISH 137

# Kiwi Lamb Burgers

*This is a mega burger so be prepared to squish it down, tuck in and get messy.*

**MAKES 4 BURGERS**

**BURGERS**
½ cup panko breadcrumbs

1 large egg, lightly beaten

2 cloves garlic, crushed

800 grams lamb mince

1 small onion, grated

2 cloves garlic, crushed

2 teaspoons ground cumin

¼ teaspoon ground cinnamon

small handful parsley, finely chopped

sea salt and ground pepper

**TO COOK AND ASSEMBLE**
oil, for cooking

4 burger buns, halved, toasted and buttered

6 slices cheddar

4 large eggs, fried

sliced tomatoes, beetroot and lettuce

good-quality egg mayonnaise, mustard or chutney, and pickles

**EQUIPMENT:** Line a baking tray.

Preheat the grill to its highest setting.

**BURGERS:** Stir the breadcrumbs, egg and garlic together in a large bowl. Add all the remaining ingredients and combine well, seasoning generously with salt and pepper. Shape into 4 patties, slightly larger than the buns as they will shrink with cooking.

**TO COOK:** Heat a little oil in a large frying pan or on a barbecue hot plate on medium and cook the patties for about 4 minutes each side, or until fully cooked through.

Place the bottom half of the burger buns on a baking tray and top each one with 1½ slices of cheese. Grill until melted.

**TO ASSEMBLE:** Top the cheesy burger bun with lettuce, then layer up with the beetroot, lamb patties, tomato, condiments, eggs and the top bun.

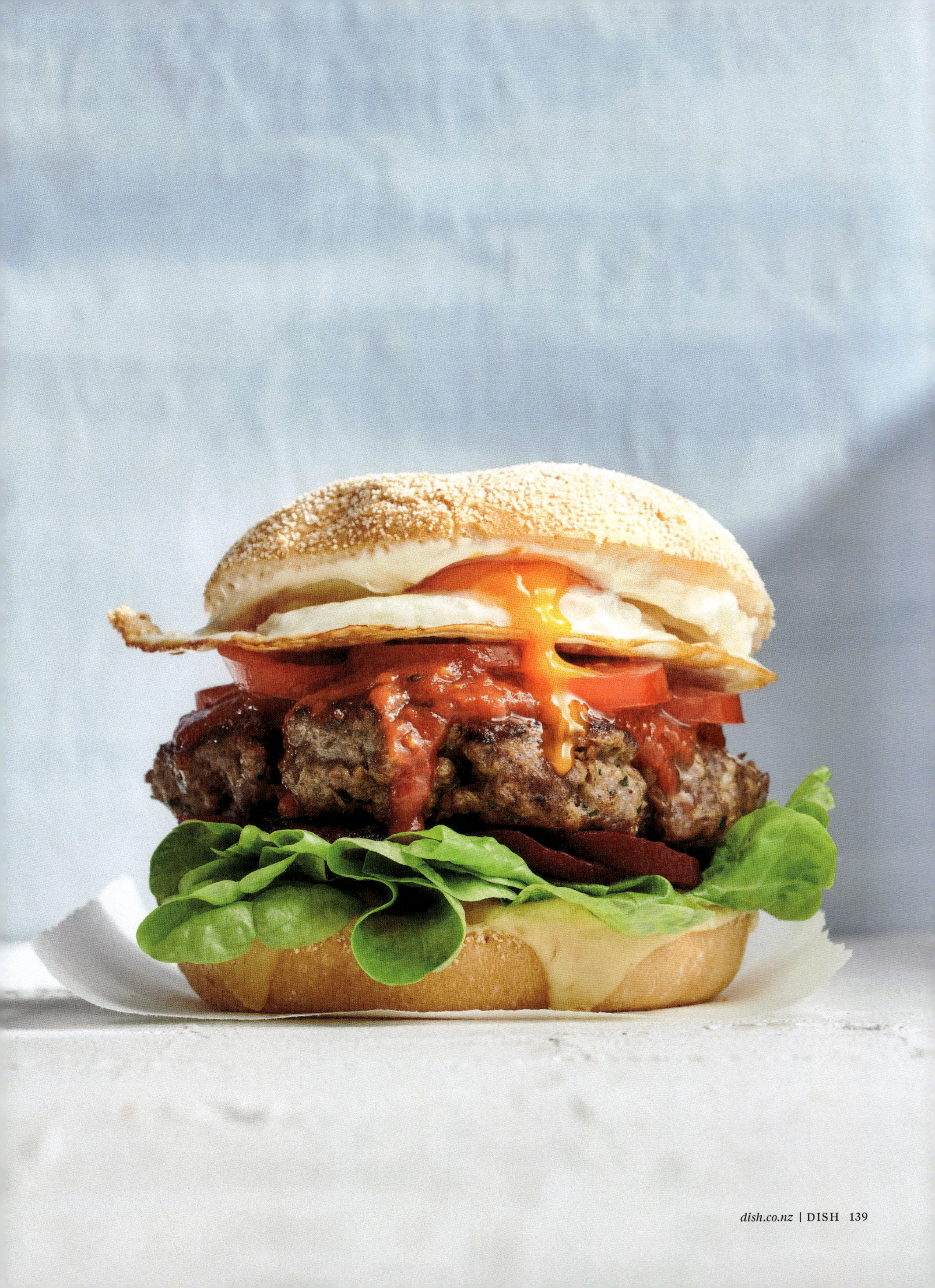

# Crispy Spiced Onion Fritter Burgers with Mango Chutney (v)

*Not your run-of-the-mill filling, these crispy, light onion fritters are sandwiched with mayo, fresh herbs and dollops of fragrant chutney in this riff on onion bhaji.*

**MAKES 4 BURGERS**

**BURGERS**

2 small red onions, thinly sliced

2 cloves garlic, crushed

1 tablespoon grated fresh ginger

¼ cup chopped coriander

½ cup plain flour

¼ teaspoon baking soda

2 teaspoons mild curry powder

½ teaspoon ground chilli

¼ teaspoon each fennel seeds and cumin seeds

1 teaspoon sea salt

¼-⅓ cup water

**TO COOK AND ASSEMBLE**

vegetable oil, for cooking

4 burger buns, halved and toasted

good-quality egg mayonnaise

purchased kasundi or tamarind or mango chutney

coriander or mint

Toss the onions, garlic, ginger and coriander together in a large bowl.

Combine the flour, baking soda, curry powder, chilli, fennel and cumin seeds and salt. Add to the onions and toss together. Sprinkle over ¼ water and mix through, adding more if needed, until it's all holding together and is quite sticky.

**TO COOK AND ASSEMBLE:** Heat 2cm of oil in a large frying pan. *A small piece of batter dropped in should sizzle and float to the surface when it is hot enough.*

Drop flattish spoonfuls of batter into the pan, making sure they're not too thick. Cook for 2 minutes, then turn and cook for a further 2 minutes. Drain on kitchen towels and sprinkle with sea salt.

Spread each bun half with mayo and chutney. Add a stack of crispy fritters and coriander or mint and sandwich together.

dish.co.nz | DISH 141

# Crispy Chicken and Bacon Burgers

*What's not to love about a chicken and bacon combo? The blue cheese mayo and pickles add a little tang while the avocado and lettuce cut the richness.*

**MAKES 4 BURGERS**

**BURGERS**

4 skinless, boneless chicken thighs

1 cup buttermilk

2 cloves garlic, crushed

sea salt and ground pepper

vegetable oil, for cooking

1 cup plain flour

1 teaspoon each baking powder, dried oregano and ground cumin

½ teaspoon ground chilli

**TO ASSEMBLE**

4 burger buns, halved, toasted and buttered

Blue Cheese Mayo (see recipe below)

8 strips streaky bacon, cooked

shredded lettuce, sliced avocado and pickles

Cut each chicken thigh into two pieces, then slash any thicker bits so they're an even thickness.

Combine the buttermilk and garlic and season with salt and pepper. Add the chicken and turn to coat. Cover and chill for at least 1 hour or up to 24 hours.

Mix the flour, baking powder, oregano, cumin and chilli in a shallow dish and season generously. Lift the chicken out of the buttermilk and coat well in the flour.

Heat 1cm of oil in a large frying pan.

Cook the chicken for about 3 minutes each side, or until fully cooked through. *Don't have the oil too hot or the crust will burn before the chicken is cooked.* Drain on kitchen towels.

**TO ASSEMBLE:** Spread the buns with Blue Cheese Mayo, then layer up with the remaining ingredients.

# Blue Cheese Mayo (gf) (v)

**MAKES 1 CUP**

⅓ cup each good-quality egg mayonnaise and sour cream

1 clove garlic, crushed

100 grams soft blue cheese, crumbled

2 teaspoons lemon juice

sea salt and ground pepper

Place all the ingredients in a food processor and blend until well combined. Season with salt and pepper.

dish.co.nz | DISH 143

# Chorizo and Garlic Prawn Burgers

*Combining fresh chorizo sausage with a good pork sausage makes for a less dense burger patty that is still packed with fabulous flavours. Add garlicky prawns and a spicy mayo and this epic burger will have you licking your fingers.*

**MAKES 4 BURGERS**

**BURGERS**
400 grams fresh chorizo sausages, skins removed

400 grams good pork sausages, skins removed

1 teaspoon dried oregano

1 teaspoon smoked paprika

½ teaspoon ground cumin

sea salt and ground pepper

**GARLIC PRAWNS**
12 large raw, peeled prawns

2 tablespoons olive oil

2 cloves garlic, crushed

**MAYO**
½ cup good-quality egg mayonnaise

1 tablespoon tomato paste

1 teaspoon each smoked paprika and lemon juice

2 teaspoons American mustard

**TO COOK AND ASSEMBLE**
oil, for cooking

1 cup grated mozzarella

4 burger buns, halved, toasted and buttered

watercress or rocket

**BURGERS:** Mix everything together until well combined. Form into 4 patties, slightly larger than the buns as they will shrink with cooking.

**PRAWNS:** Cut the prawns in half to give you two thinner halves, or leave them whole if using smaller prawns. Toss with the oil and garlic, then cover and chill.

**MAYO:** Stir everything together in a bowl, then set aside.

**TO COOK AND ASSEMBLE:** Heat a little oil in a frying pan or on a barbecue hot plate on high. Season the prawns, tip into the pan or onto the barbecue and cook until pink. Remove, cover and set aside.

Wipe the pan or barbecue hot plate and heat a little more oil on a medium heat. Cook the patties for 4 minutes then turn over and top with the mozzarella. Cover and cook for another 2-3 minutes, until the cheese has melted and the burgers are fully cooked through.

**TO SERVE:** Spread the buns with the mayo and layer up with the patties, prawns and greens.

dish.co.nz | DISH 145

# Moroccan Lamb Burgers, Grilled Haloumi and Pistachio Salsa

*Spiked with aromatic herbs and topped with grilled haloumi and a fragrant salsa, this could easily be your star summer burger.*

**MAKES 4 BURGERS**

**BURGERS**

1 cup panko breadcrumbs

⅓ cup milk

2 cloves garlic, crushed

1 teaspoon each ground cumin and sweet smoked paprika

½ teaspoon ground cinnamon

1 large egg, beaten

big handful fresh coriander, finely chopped

600 grams lamb mince

sea salt and ground pepper

**SALSA**

½ cup pistachios

½ cup each packed basil and mint

2 cloves garlic, crushed

1 tablespoon lemon juice

1 teaspoon sea salt

⅓ cup olive oil

**TO SERVE**

200 grams haloumi, sliced

4 hamburger buns, halved and toasted

purchased kasundi or other tomato relish, rocket, strips of cucumber and thick plain yoghurt, to serve

**BURGERS:** Combine all the ingredients except the lamb, salt and pepper in a large bowl and leave for 5 minutes. Add the lamb, season and mix well. Form 4 patties slightly larger than the buns, as they will shrink with cooking. Chill until ready to cook, but remove from the fridge 30 minutes before cooking.

**SALSA:** Put half the pistachios and all the remaining ingredients in a food processor and blend until well chopped but not totally smooth. Roughly chop the remaining pistachios and stir through.

**TO COOK AND SERVE:** Heat a little oil in a frying pan or on a barbecue hot plate on medium and cook for 4-5 minutes each side, or until cooked through. Heat a little more oil and cook the haloumi on both sides until golden. Spread the bottom bun with tomato relish and layer up with rocket, cucumber, a patty and haloumi. Top with a spoonful of yoghurt and a dollop of the salsa. Add the tops and serve immediately.

dish.co.nz | DISH 147

# Beef and Smoked Cheddar Burgers

*The two most important tips for a great burger: use really good-quality beef mince with a decent fat content, and don't work the mixture too much otherwise you'll end up with a dense, hard burger instead of a big juicy one!*

**SERVES 4**

**BURGER**

800 grams good-quality beef mince

2 tablespoons tomato paste

2 tablespoons oyster sauce

1 teaspoon sesame oil

2 cloves garlic, crushed

2 large egg yolks

sea salt and ground pepper

**TO COOK AND ASSEMBLE**

oil, for cooking

8 slices smoked cheddar

4 buns, halved and toasted

good-quality egg mayonnaise

crisp lettuce leaves

sliced tomatoes

12 slices streaky bacon, cooked till crisp

Beer and Hoisin-braised Onions (optional, see recipe page 210)

**BURGER:** Place all the ingredients in a bowl, season with salt and pepper and gently but thoroughly mix together. Shape into 4 patties slightly larger than the buns, as they will shrink with cooking. Chill until ready to cook, but remove from the fridge 30 minutes before cooking.

**TO COOK AND ASSEMBLE:** Heat a little oil in a frying pan or on a barbecue hot plate on medium and cook the patties for 4 minutes on the first side. Turn over and cook for a further 2-3 minutes, then top with the cheddar. Cover and cook until the cheese has melted and the burgers are just cooked through. Spread the buns with mayonnaise, then top with lettuce, tomato, the beef patties, 3 slices of bacon each and Beer and Hoisin-braised Onions, if using.

*dish.co.nz* | DISH 149

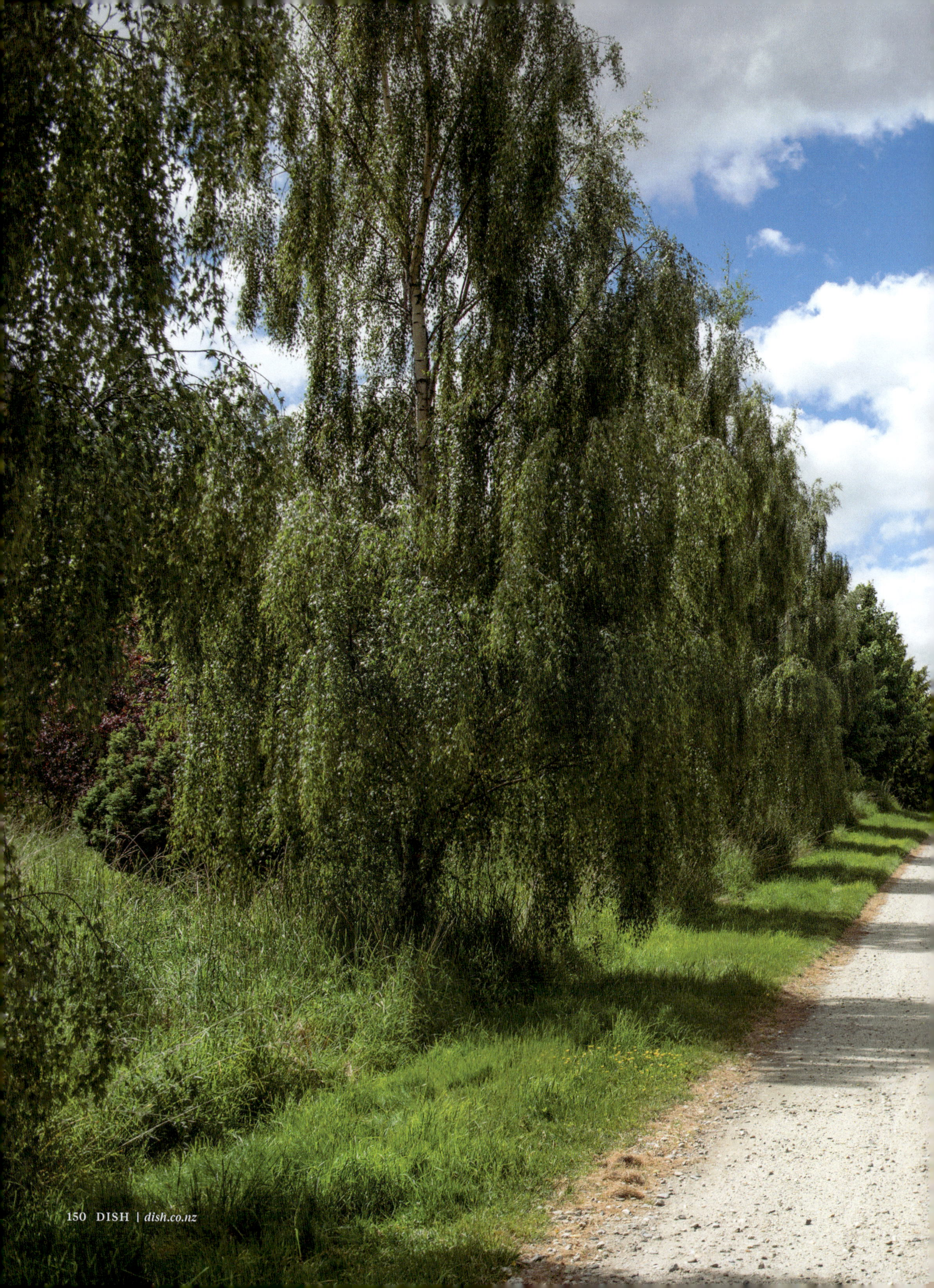

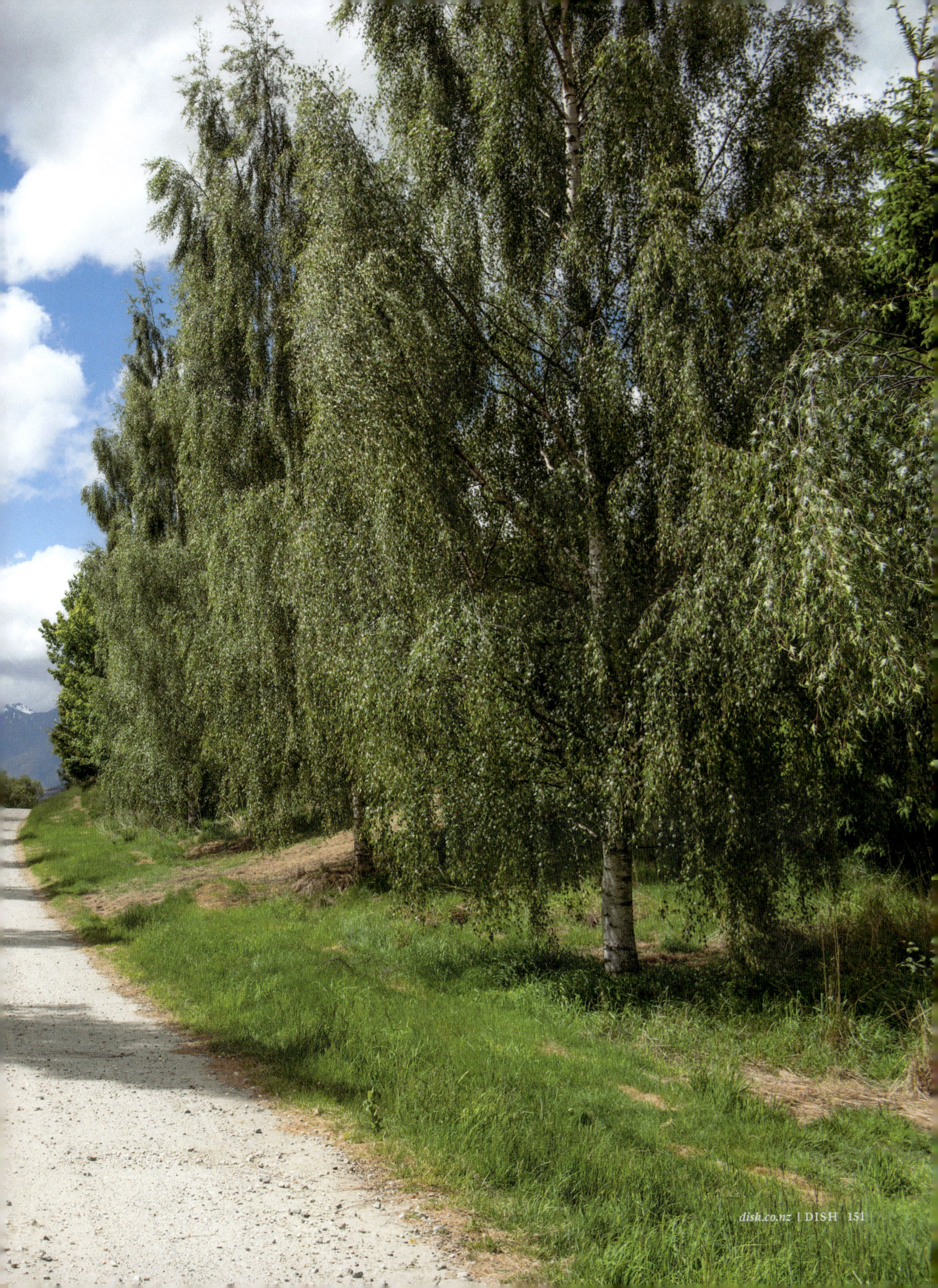

# WHAT'S FOR DESSERT?

*After the main event, it's always nice to finish the evening with dessert, but in summer we're leaving behind the stodgy mid-winter puds and kicking into gear with summertime tarts, ice creams and fruity delights. Making the most of the season's bounty, we have Rhubarb and Strawberry Frangipane Tarts (page 168), Boozy Barbecued Stone Fruit Parcels (page 164) and Summer Fruits in a Lemongrass and Citrus Syrup (page 166). To cool down in style, there's Luscious Baklava and Pistachio Ice Cream (page 154) and stunning Lemon Meringue and Blueberry Pie Ice Cream (page 162). And if you're after a total showstopper, you can't go past the Tiramisu Espresso Martini No-bake Cheesecake (page 178).*

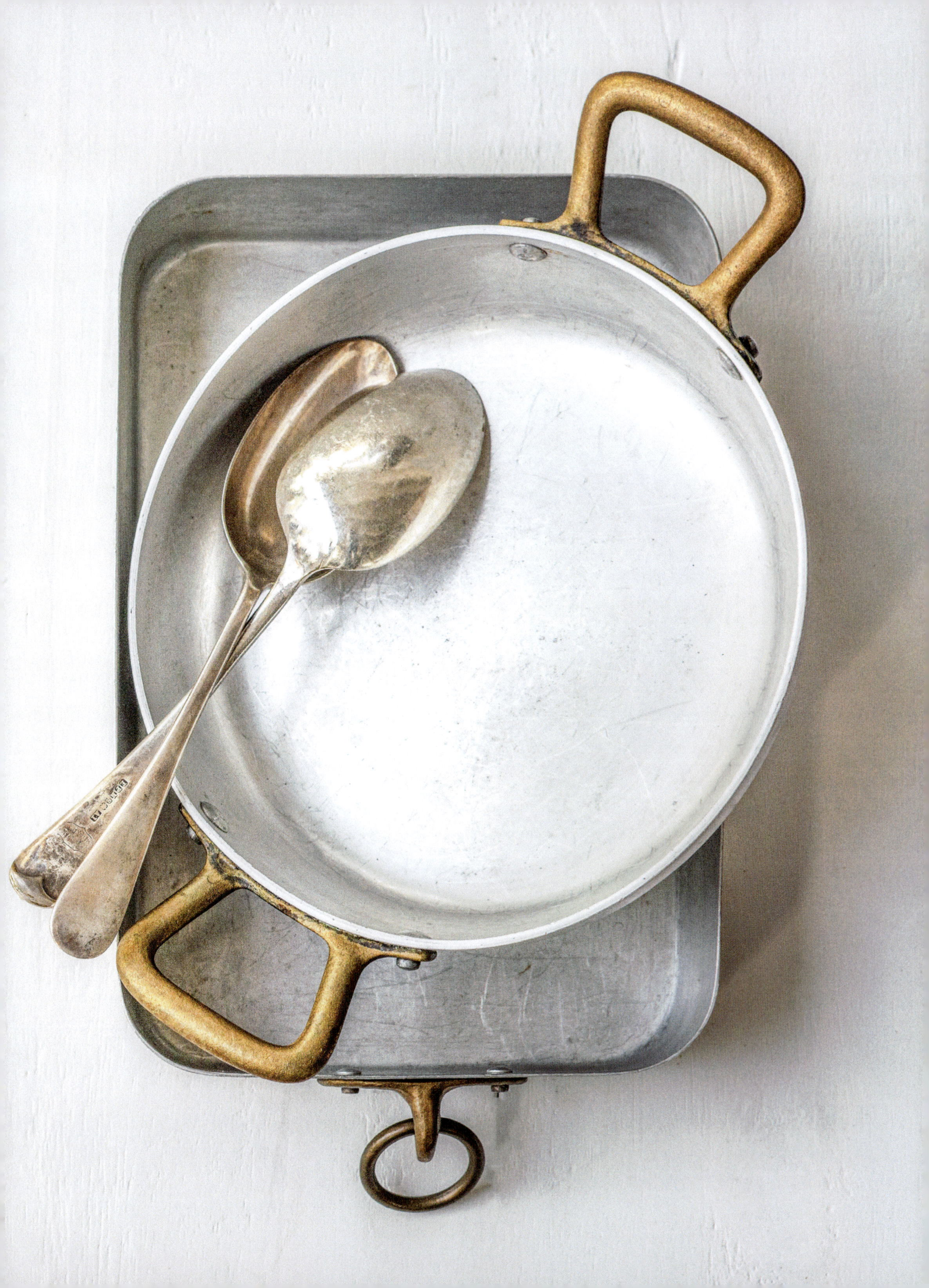

# Luscious Baklava and Pistachio Ice Cream

*A fun summer spin on a Mediterranean favourite! Delicious nuggets of sticky-sweet-crisp baklava and vibrant crunchy pistachios are folded through rich, creamy vanilla bean ice cream for a super easy and totally delicious dessert.*

**MAKES 1 LITRE**

1 litre good-quality vanilla bean ice cream

⅓ cup chopped pistachios

4-6 pieces of baklava, roughly chopped (see Cook's note)

**EQUIPMENT:** 1½ litre-capacity freezer-safe container.

Leave the ice cream at room temperature until semi-soft. Transfer half the ice cream to the container and drop half the baklava and half the pistachios over the top. Cover with the remaining ice cream, baklava and pistachios (don't press the topping down). Cover with plastic wrap and re-freeze for several hours. Scoop into bowls to serve.

**COOK'S NOTE:** Baklava can be purchased at specialty food stores and Middle Eastern shops. Pieces come in various sizes, so buy 6 if they are small. You want a generous amount in the ice cream.

dish.co.nz | DISH 155

# Chilled Espresso Martini Affogato (gf)

*Channel the flavours of a classic espresso martini into this simple dessert. Pour the chilled martini over rich coffee ice cream and top with roasted nuts and chocolate-coated coffee beans. Elegant, decadent and a guaranteed crowd-pleaser.*

**MAKES 1**

1-2 scoops purchased coffee ice cream

¼ cup vodka

¼ cup espresso coffee, cooled

¼ cup Kahlúa

1 tablespoon chopped roasted hazelnuts

chocolate-coated coffee beans, to garnish

Put the ice cream into a chilled martini glass.

Vigorously shake the vodka, Kahlúa and espresso in a cocktail shaker with a few ice cubes. Pour over the ice cream and scatter with the hazelnuts and coffee beans. Devour immediately.

dish.co.nz | DISH 157

# Olive Oil and Orange Cake with Honey-roasted Apricots

*Olive oil adds a lot of moisture to this cake and I love to use a fruity version for extra flavour. It keeps well in an airtight container, without the cream and fruit topping, for 5 days.*

**SERVES 8**

¾ cup olive oil

1 cup caster sugar

3 large eggs

½ cup milk

1 teaspoon vanilla extract

½ teaspoon sea salt

finely grated zest 1 orange

1½ cups ground almonds (almond meal)

1 cup plain flour

1 teaspoon baking powder

1 teaspoon baking soda

½ teaspoon each ground cinnamon, ground cardamom and ground nutmeg

**TO SERVE**

1 cup mascarpone

1 cup cream

Honey Roasted Apricots (see recipe 213)

⅓ cup sliced almonds, toasted

**EQUIPMENT:** Grease a 20cm springform cake tin and line the base and sides with baking paper.

Preheat the oven to 160°C regular bake.

Whisk the olive oil, sugar, eggs, milk, vanilla, salt and orange zest together in a large bowl. Combine the ground almonds, flour, baking powder, baking soda and all the spices together, then whisk into the olive oil mixture until smooth.

Pour into the tin and bake for 30 minutes. Loosely tent with a piece of foil and bake for a further 35 minutes, or until the cake feels firm to the touch and a skewer inserted into the centre comes out clean. Set aside to cool completely in the tin.

**TO SERVE:** Whisk the mascarpone and cream together to form soft peaks. Place the cake on a serving plate and spoon over half of the cream.

Top with some of the apricots and scatter over the almonds, serving the remaining apricots and cream separately.

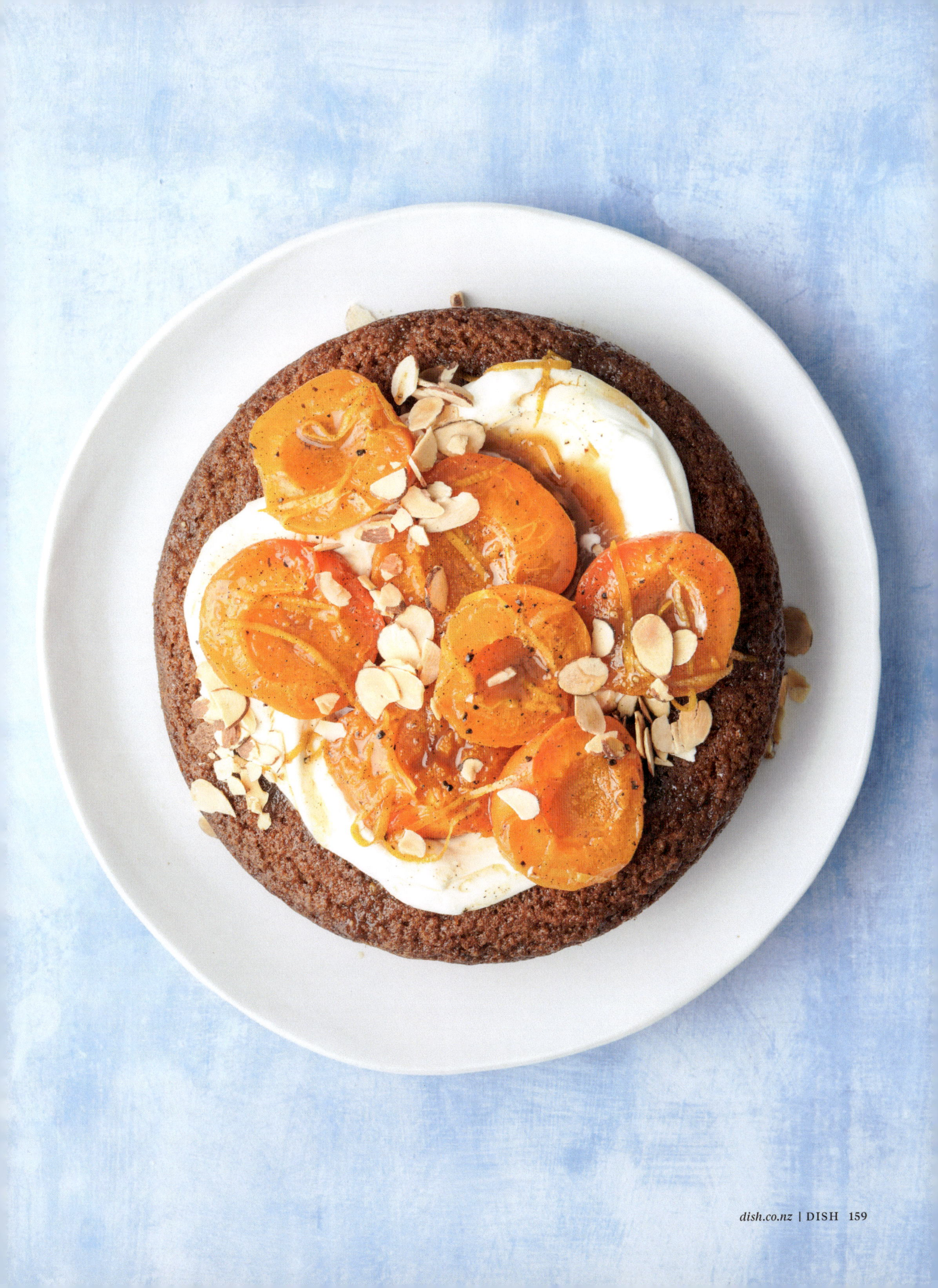

# Rockmelon and Gin Slushies (gf)

*The perfect frozen cocktail dessert for warm balmy evenings. You can use whatever gin you have on hand and create your own slushie flavour profile!*

**SERVES 2-3 DEPENDING ON THE SIZE OF THE GLASSES**

1 medium very ripe rockmelon, peeled and coarsely chopped, plus extra to garnish, if desired

**SIMPLE SYRUP**

½ cup sugar

½ cup water

juice 1 orange

1 long red chilli, thinly sliced

2 sprigs mint

**TO SERVE**
chilled gin, to taste

**MELON:** Spread the melon on a tray lined with plastic wrap and chill in the freezer until frozen, preferably overnight.

**SYRUP:** Place all the ingredients in a small saucepan and bring to the boil, stirring to dissolve the sugar. Cool, then cover and chill until ready to use.

**TO SERVE:** Put the frozen melon, ¼ cup of the strained simple syrup and gin to taste in a high-speed blender. Whizz until smooth, adding more syrup if needed to get the desired consistency. Immediately spoon into well-chilled sundae glasses. Decorate with extra slices of rockmelon, if desired.

**COOK'S NOTE:** If you want the simple syrup to have a spicy kick, leave the sliced chilli in until ready to use. For a regular syrup, leave out the chilli and just use the mint leaves.

dish.co.nz | DISH 161

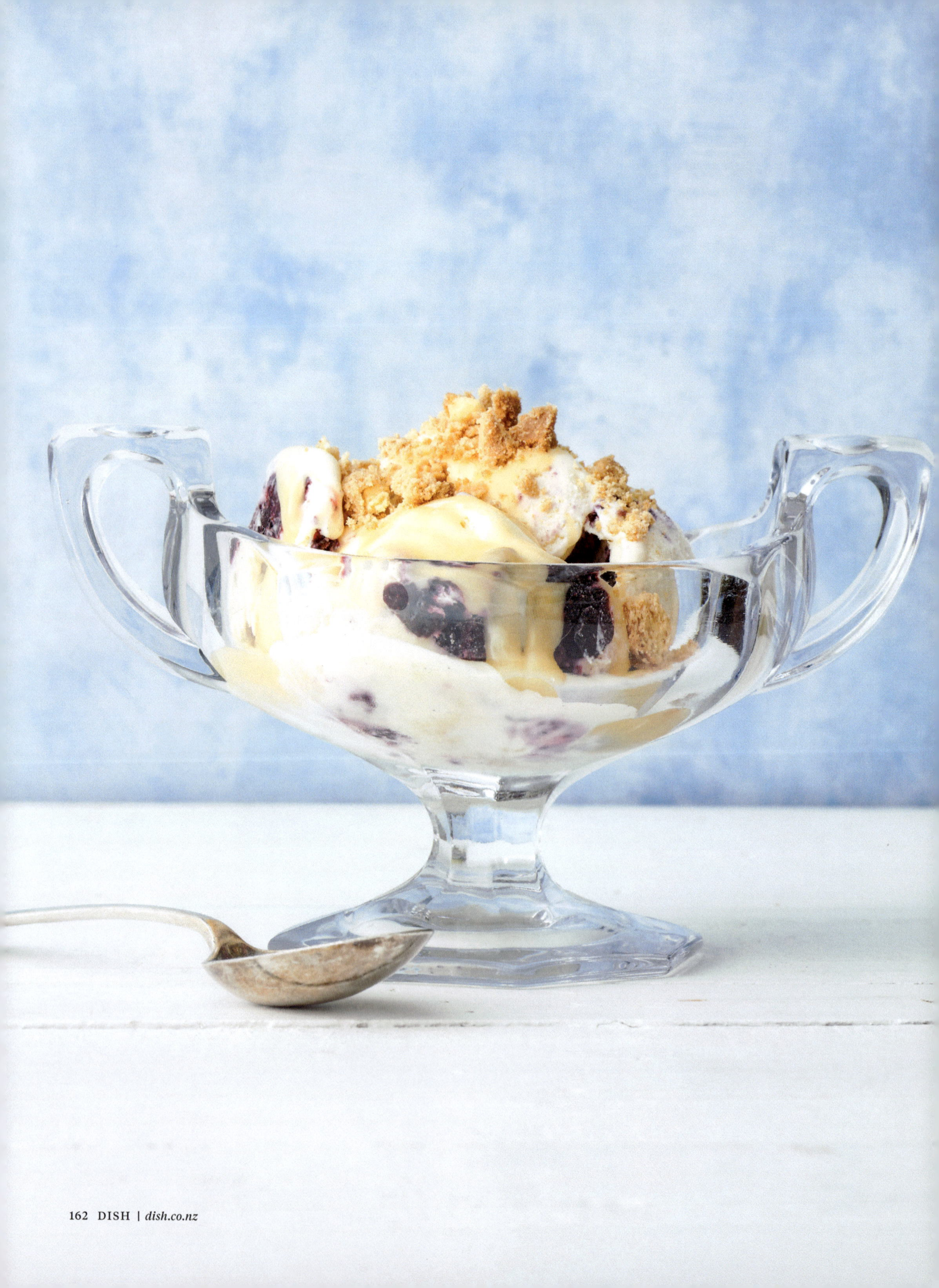

# Lemon Meringue and Blueberry Pie Ice Cream

*Get creative with your ice cream sundae combinations! Fresh, citrusy lemon curd, chunks of buttery shortbread and juicy blueberry jam make a fun, summery and totally irresistible sundae.*

**SERVES 6**

**BLUEBERRY CHIA JAM**
250 grams blueberries

2 tablespoons honey or maple syrup

1 tablespoon lemon juice

1 teaspoon vanilla extract

1½ tablespoons black chia seeds

**ICE CREAM**
1 litre good-quality vanilla bean ice cream

250 grams purchased shortbread, roughly crumbled

1½ cups purchased lemon curd

**EQUIPMENT:** 1½ litre-capacity freezer-safe container.

**BLUEBERRY CHIA JAM:** Put the blueberries, honey, lemon juice and vanilla in a small saucepan and bring to the boil. Reduce the heat and cook, stirring occasionally, for about 10 minutes, or until the berries have burst and there's lots of juice.

Take off the heat, sprinkle over the chia seeds and stir well, ensuring there are no clumps of chia seeds in the jam.

Cool, then store in a sealed container in the fridge for up to 10 days.

**ICE CREAM:** Leave the ice cream at room temperature until semi-soft. Set aside 50 grams of the shortbread crumbs and ⅓ cup of the lemon curd for serving.

Transfer half the ice cream to the container and dollop over half each of the lemon curd, shortbread and blueberry chia jam and gently marble them through. Repeat with the rest of the ice cream to make another layer. Cover with plastic wrap and re-freeze for several hours.

Scoop into bowls to serve and top with the reserved lemon curd and crumbs.

# Boozy Barbecued Stone Fruit Parcels

*This recipe gives you the basic ingredients for making one parcel and it's quite a generous serving. I've used stone fruit, but use whatever fruit is in season and best on the day.*

**MAKES 1 GENEROUS PARCEL**

**FRUIT**
1 peach

1 nectarine

2 apricots

2 plums

**PARCELS**
3 gingernut biscuits, roughly broken

1 tablespoon whisky (or use your own favourite tipple)

1-2 tablespoons honey, depending on the ripeness of the fruit

1 teaspoon orange zest

1 tablespoon orange juice

⅓ piece vanilla bean, split with seeds scraped out, or use ¼ teaspoon vanilla extract

2 teaspoons butter

**EQUIPMENT:** Cut out a 20cm x 20cm piece each of baking paper and foil.

**FRUIT:** Halve and stone the fruit, cutting any larger pieces into quarters.

**PARCELS:** Place the baking paper over the foil and scatter over the biscuits. Arrange the fruit over the biscuits. Stir together the whisky, honey, zest, juice and vanilla bean seeds or extract and pour over the fruit. Nestle in the vanilla bean and dot over the butter. Bring the sides together and fold to seal tightly. Place on a heated barbecue and cook for 15-20 minutes, or until the fruit is tender.

**TO SERVE:** Open the parcel and serve with a scoop of ice cream, runny cream or yoghurt.

**COOK'S NOTE:** The parcels can also be cooked in the oven. Preheat the oven to 190°C fan bake, place the parcels on an oven tray and bake for 15-20 minutes.

dish.co.nz | DISH 165

# Summer Fruits in a Lemongrass and Citrus Syrup (gf)

*This zesty syrup will go with a wide range of fruits: cherries, pineapple, melons, berries and oranges are all delicious.*

**SERVES 4**

**SYRUP**
¼ cup orange juice

¼ cup lime juice

¼ cup maple syrup

2 stalks lemongrass, thinly sliced

2 whole star anise

1 cinnamon stick

**FRUIT**
1 mango, peeled, halved and cut into wedges

4 ripe apricots, cut into wedges

4 plums, cut into wedges

**TO SERVE**
purchased coconut sorbet

mint leaves

**SYRUP:** Put all the syrup ingredients in a small saucepan and bring to the boil. Simmer for 2 minutes, then cool, cover and chill.

**FRUIT:** Place the fruit in a bowl and strain over the syrup. Leave for 30 minutes for the fruit to mingle with the syrup.

**TO SERVE:** Divide the fruit and syrup among glasses or bowls and top with a scoop of coconut sorbet and a few mint leaves.

*dish.co.nz* | DISH 167

168 DISH | *dish.co.nz*

# Rhubarb and Strawberry Frangipane Tarts

*These vibrant, rustic beauties are brilliant warm or at room temperature.*

**SERVES 6**

**FRUIT**
350 grams rhubarb, washed and chopped into 4cm lengths

1 tablespoon vanilla extract

2 tablespoons caster sugar

250 grams strawberries, halved

**PASTRY**
350 grams good-quality butter puff pastry

**FRANGIPANE**
50 grams butter, at room temperature

⅓ cup caster sugar

1¼ cups ground almonds (almond meal)

1 tablespoon plain flour

1 large egg

1 teaspoon vanilla extract

**TO SERVE**
2 tablespoons strawberry jam

vanilla bean ice cream

**EQUIPMENT:** Grease 6 x 12cm loose-based tart tins.

Preheat the oven to 180°C regular bake.

**FRUIT:** Put the rhubarb in a roasting dish and add the vanilla and caster sugar. Toss to combine, spread out into a single layer and roast for 10-12 minutes. Add the strawberries and toss very gently, then cook for another 5 minutes. Remove from the oven and allow to cool in the juices.

**PASTRY:** Cut 6 circles of pastry slightly larger than the tart tins. Press the pastry into the tins, then prick the bases well with a fork and pop in the freezer while preparing the frangipane.

**FRANGIPANE:** Put the butter, sugar, almonds and flour in a food processor and whizz to combine. Add the egg and vanilla and whizz again until smooth.

Cut 6 circles of baking paper and place in the pastry shells. Fill with baking beans, weights or rice and bake for 10 minutes. Remove the baking paper and weights and bake for a further 5 minutes. Poke down the middles of the pastry shells (which will have puffed up) with the back of a teaspoon and reduce the oven temperature to 170°C.

Fill the tart shells with frangipane, then, draining the fruit as you go, place it on top. Bake for a further 8-10 minutes. Remove from the oven and allow to cool before removing from the tins.

**TO SERVE:** The tarts can be either briefly reheated in the oven or served at room temperature. Just before serving, heat the jam for 30 seconds in the microwave and brush over the fruit. Serve with ice cream.

# Spiced Pumpkin Cheesecake Tart

*My dad's favourite, this is a perfectly spiced semi-classic.*

**SERVES 10**

**PASTRY**
100 grams cold butter, chopped

¼ cup icing sugar

1¼ cups plain flour

1 large egg yolk

½-1 tablespoon iced water

**FILLING**
600 grams peeled, deseeded pumpkin, cut into 6cm chunks

3 tablespoons maple syrup

500 grams cream cheese, at room temperature

1¼ cups caster sugar

1 tablespoon ground cinnamon

¼ teaspoon each ground nutmeg, ground cloves and ground allspice

2 teaspoons ground ginger

¼ teaspoon sea salt

1 tablespoon custard powder

3 large eggs

**TO SERVE**
Walnut Praline (see recipe page 220)

softly whipped cream

**EQUIPMENT:** Grease a deep 25cm loose-based tart tin. Line a roasting dish and a square lipped oven tray with baking paper.

Preheat the oven to 180°C regular bake.

**PASTRY:** Whizz the butter, icing sugar and flour in a food processor until the mixture resembles breadcrumbs. Add the yolk and ½ tablespoon water. Pulse until it forms large clumps, adding the remaining water only if necessary. Tip out onto a clean bench and pat into a disc. Wrap in plastic wrap and refrigerate for 15 minutes.

**FILLING:** Place the pumpkin in the roasting dish, drizzle with 2 tablespoons of the maple syrup, then cover with foil. Bake for 45 minutes, or until tender. Cool.

Roll out the chilled pastry out to a circle slightly larger than the tart tin. Press into the tin, patch up any tears and trim the edges. Prick the base with a fork and pop in the freezer for 5 minutes. Line the pastry with baking paper, fill with baking weights or rice and bake for 12 minutes. Remove the paper and weights and bake for a further 8 minutes. Meanwhile, whizz the cooled pumpkin, remaining maple syrup, cream cheese, sugar, spices, salt and custard powder in a food processor until smooth. Add the eggs and pulse briefly to combine, then pour into the pastry case. Tap the tin on the bench to pop any air bubbles, then bake for 35-40 minutes, or until there is just a slight wobble in the middle. Cool completely on the bench, then place in the fridge to chill.

**TO SERVE:** Serve the tart topped with the Walnut Praline, alongside plenty of softly whipped cream.

dish.co.nz | DISH 171

# Classic Lemon Tart

*This has long been my ultimate go-to tart – simple perfection.*

**SERVES 8-10**

**PASTRY**
110 grams cold butter, chopped

1⅓ cups plain flour

⅓ cup icing sugar

finely grated zest 1 lemon

1 large egg yolk

1-2 teaspoons iced water

**FILLING**
4 large eggs

1 large egg yolk

¾ cup caster sugar

250ml cream

250ml freshly squeezed lemon juice

**EQUIPMENT:** Lightly grease a 25cm loose-based tart tin.

Preheat the oven to 180°C regular bake.

**PASTRY:** Pulse the butter, flour, sugar and zest in a food processor to combine, then add the egg yolk and 1 teaspoon iced water. Pulse until the mixture starts coming together, adding the remaining water only if necessary. Tip out onto a clean bench and pat into a disc. Wrap in plastic wrap and refrigerate for 30 minutes.

Remove the pastry from the fridge, let it sit for 5 minutes, then roll out on a lightly floured surface until it is 5cm bigger than the tart tin. Use a fish slice to slip it off the bench and into the tin. Press firmly into the base and sides and prick the base with a fork. Put in the freezer for 10 minutes.

**FILLING:** Whisk the eggs, yolk, sugar and cream together. *Don't whisk too hard or you will make it bubbly; gently does it.*

Line the pastry with baking paper, fill with baking weights or rice and bake for 12 minutes. Remove the paper and weights and bake for a further 10 minutes. Put the tart case on a baking tray and return to the oven. Working quickly, stir the lemon juice into the filling, then pour the filling through a sieve into a jug and carefully pour it straight into the case in the oven. Reduce the oven temperature to 150°C and bake for 25-30 minutes, until just set, but still with a bit of wobble in the middle. Cool in the tin.

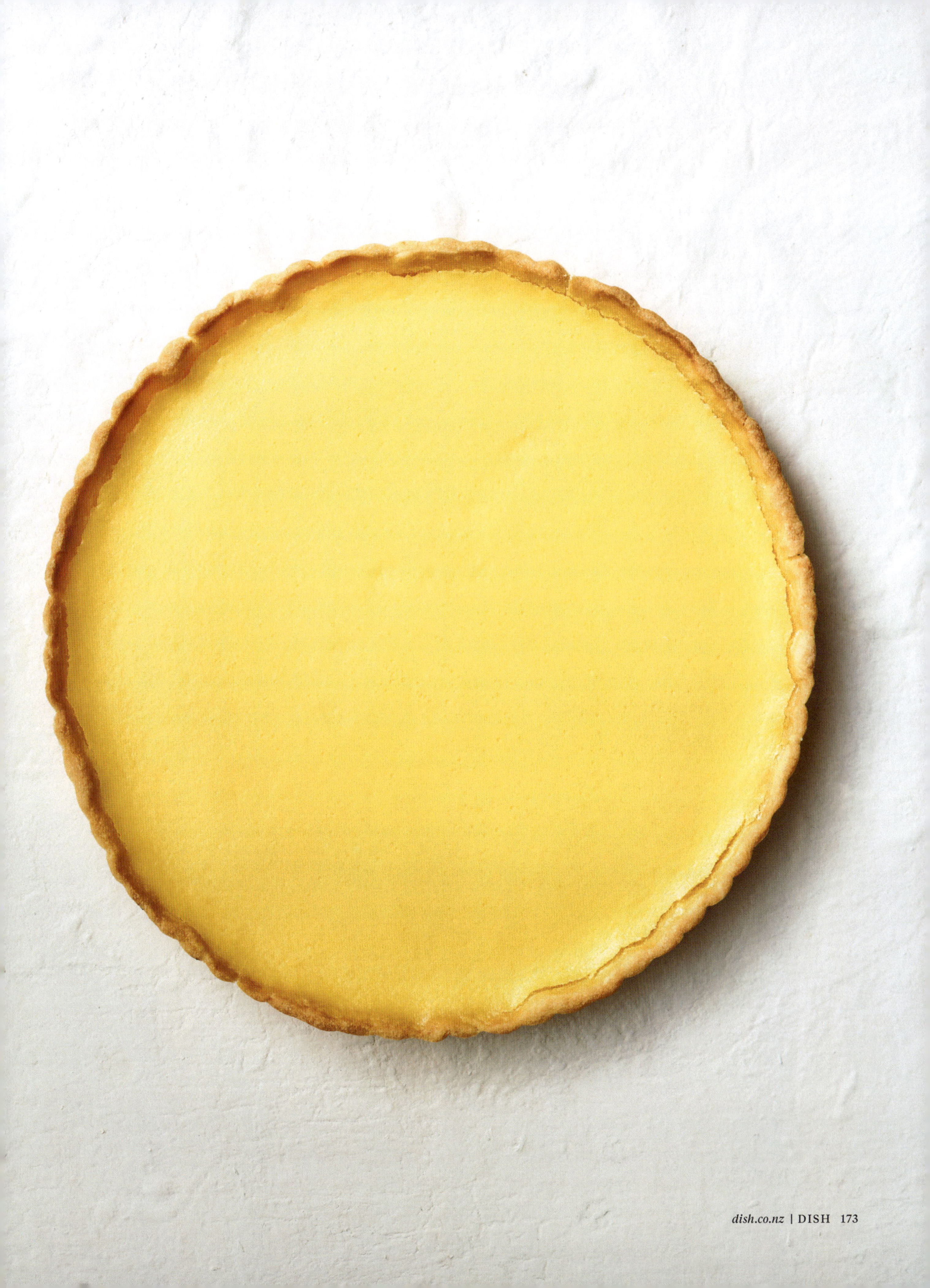

# Double Chocolate, Roasted Peanut and Tahini Skillet Cookie (gf)

*Desserts don't come easier than this delicious creation. Make sure you don't over-bake it; it's better a bit under so it's all tender with melty chocolate.*

**SERVES 4-6**

¼ cup sunflower oil

½ cup coconut sugar

¼ cup tahini

2 large eggs

1 teaspoon vanilla extract

½ cup ground almonds (almond meal)

½ cup gluten-free flour

¼ teaspoon baking soda

⅓ cup roasted peanuts, roughly chopped

⅓ cup each white and dark chocolate drops

¼ teaspoon sea salt

**EQUIPMENT:** Lightly grease a 20cm ovenproof frying pan or baking dish and line with baking paper.

Preheat the oven to 160°C fan bake.

Whisk the oil, sugar, tahini, eggs and vanilla together in a large bowl. Whisk together the almonds, flour and baking soda, then stir into the egg mixture along with the peanuts and half each of the white and dark chocolate drops.

Spread the dough evenly in the pan, then scatter over the remaining chocolate drops and the sea salt.

Bake for about 18 minutes, or until just baked but still slightly soft when pressed with your fingertips. *Cooking time will depend on the depth of your baking dish.* Remove from the oven and cool for 5 minutes.

**TO SERVE:** Scoop into bowls and serve with cream, mascarpone or ice cream.

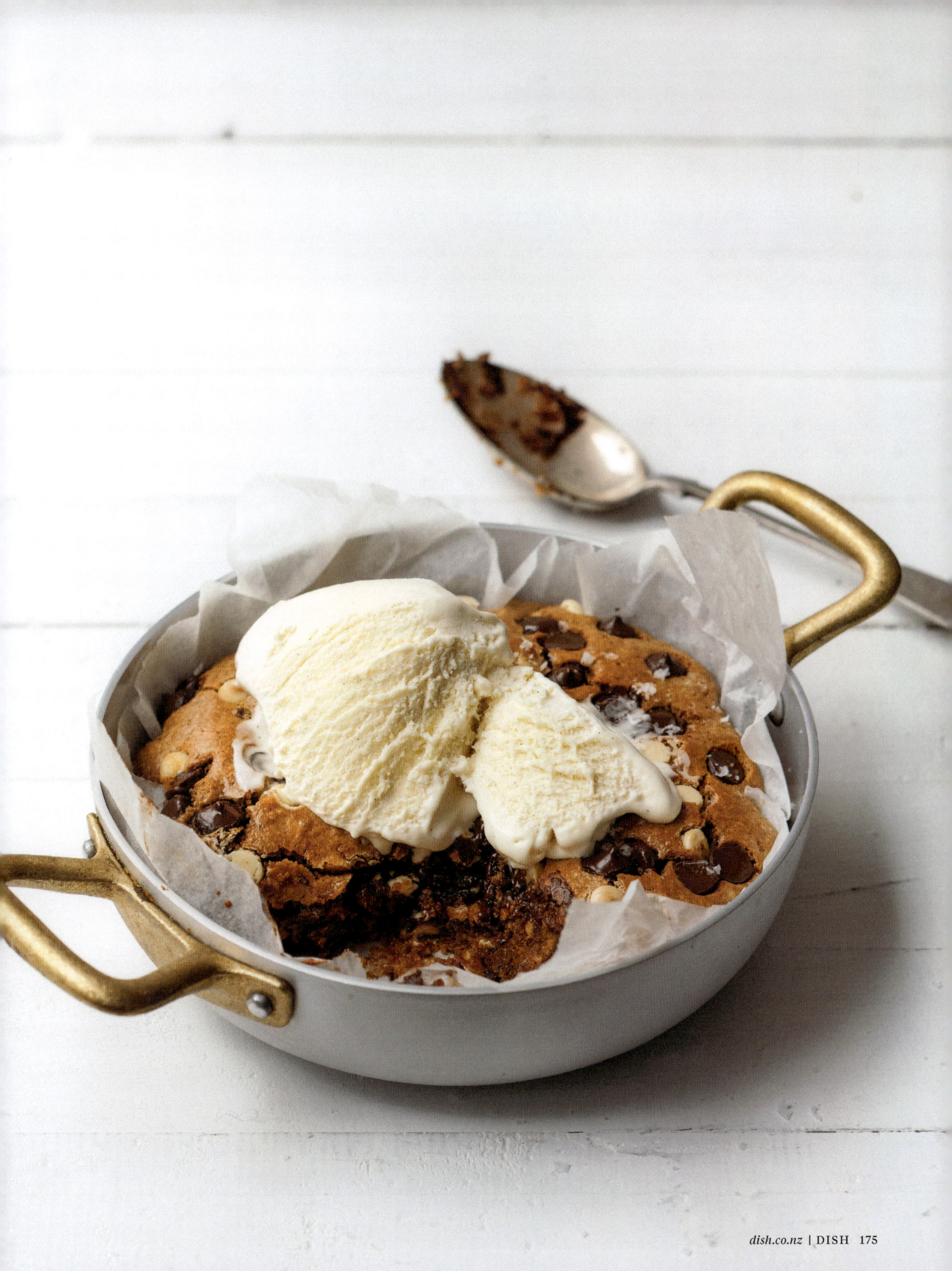

# Macadamia Caramel Tart

*This is so incredibly simple to make, but looks totally fabulous, and tastes even better – caramelly, nutty goodness!*

**SERVES 8-10**

**PASTRY**
80 grams cold butter, chopped

¼ cup brown sugar

1¼ cups plain flour

1 large egg yolk

1 teaspoon iced water

**FILLING**
1 tablespoon butter

200 grams sweetened condensed milk (half a tin)

395-gram tin caramel sweetened condensed milk (or dulce de leche)

2 tablespoons golden syrup

1½ cups roasted, salted macadamias

½ teaspoon sea salt

**TO SERVE**
vanilla bean ice cream

Salted Caramel Sauce (see recipe page 216)

**EQUIPMENT:** 5cm-deep, 20cm loose-based tart tin.

Preheat the oven to 180°C regular bake.

**PASTRY:** Put the butter, brown sugar and flour in a food processor and pulse until the mixture resembles breadcrumbs. Add the yolk and half the water. Pulse until the dough starts coming together, adding the remaining water only if necessary. Tip out onto a clean bench and pat into a disc. Wrap in plastic wrap and refrigerate for 20 minutes.

Roll out the pastry to a circle slightly larger than the tart tin. Ease into the tin, patch up any tears and trim the edges. Prick the base with a fork and pop back in the fridge for 10 minutes. Line the pastry with baking paper, fill with baking weights or rice and bake for 12 minutes. Remove the paper and weights and bake for a further 5 minutes.

While the pastry is cooking, put the butter, condensed milks and syrup in a large microwave-safe bowl. Heat in 3 x 30-second bursts, then whisk until smooth. Heat for a further 30 seconds if necessary. Put the nuts in the parbaked pastry case, then pour over the filling. Bake for 20-25 minutes, until golden and set. Sprinkle over the sea salt. Leave to cool in the tin, then remove.

**TO SERVE:** Serve at room temperature with ice cream and Salted Caramel Sauce.

dish.co.nz | DISH 177

# Tiramisu Espresso Martini No-bake Cheesecake

*Wait, what? Yes, you read correctly... and soooo good!*

**SERVES 10-12**

**BASE**
90 grams melted butter

1 tablespoon instant espresso

250 grams plain chocolate biscuits

**FILLING**
2 tablespoons instant espresso

120ml Kahlúa

10 Savoiardi biscuits

4 sheets Equagold Gold gelatine

250 grams mascarpone

500 grams cream cheese, at room temperature

1 cup caster sugar

1 large egg yolk

1 tablespoon vanilla bean paste

**TOPPING**
1 cup cream

1 teaspoon vanilla bean paste

250 grams mascarpone

80 grams dark chocolate, finely grated

**EQUIPMENT:** Grease a 23cm springform cake tin and line the base and sides with baking paper.

**BASE:** Mix the melted butter and espresso granules together, then add to a food processor along with the chocolate biscuits and whizz until the mixture resembles wet sand. Pour into the prepared tin and use the base of a glass to press it into the base and sides. Put in the fridge to chill.

**FILLING:** Whisk the espresso granules and Kahlúa together in a small bowl. Briefly dip each Savoiardi biscuit in the Kahlúa mixture and place in a single layer on the base. *You will need to break a few biscuits in half to completely cover the base.* Refrigerate until needed. Strain the remaining liquid into a microwave-safe bowl.

Put the gelatine sheets in a bowl of cold water for 5 minutes. Whizz the mascarpone, cream cheese, sugar, egg yolk and vanilla together in a food processor. Heat the reserved Kahlúa liquid in the microwave until hot – about 45 seconds on high. Remove the gelatine from the water and squeeze out any liquid. Add to the hot Kahlúa mixture and whisk until dissolved. Add the gelatine mixture to the cream cheese mixture, then whizz until smooth. Pour over the Savoiardi-lined base and chill for at least 2 hours, or up to overnight.

**TOPPING:** Whisk the cream to firm peaks, then whisk in the vanilla and mascarpone. Top the cheesecake with the cream mixture and sprinkle with chocolate to serve.

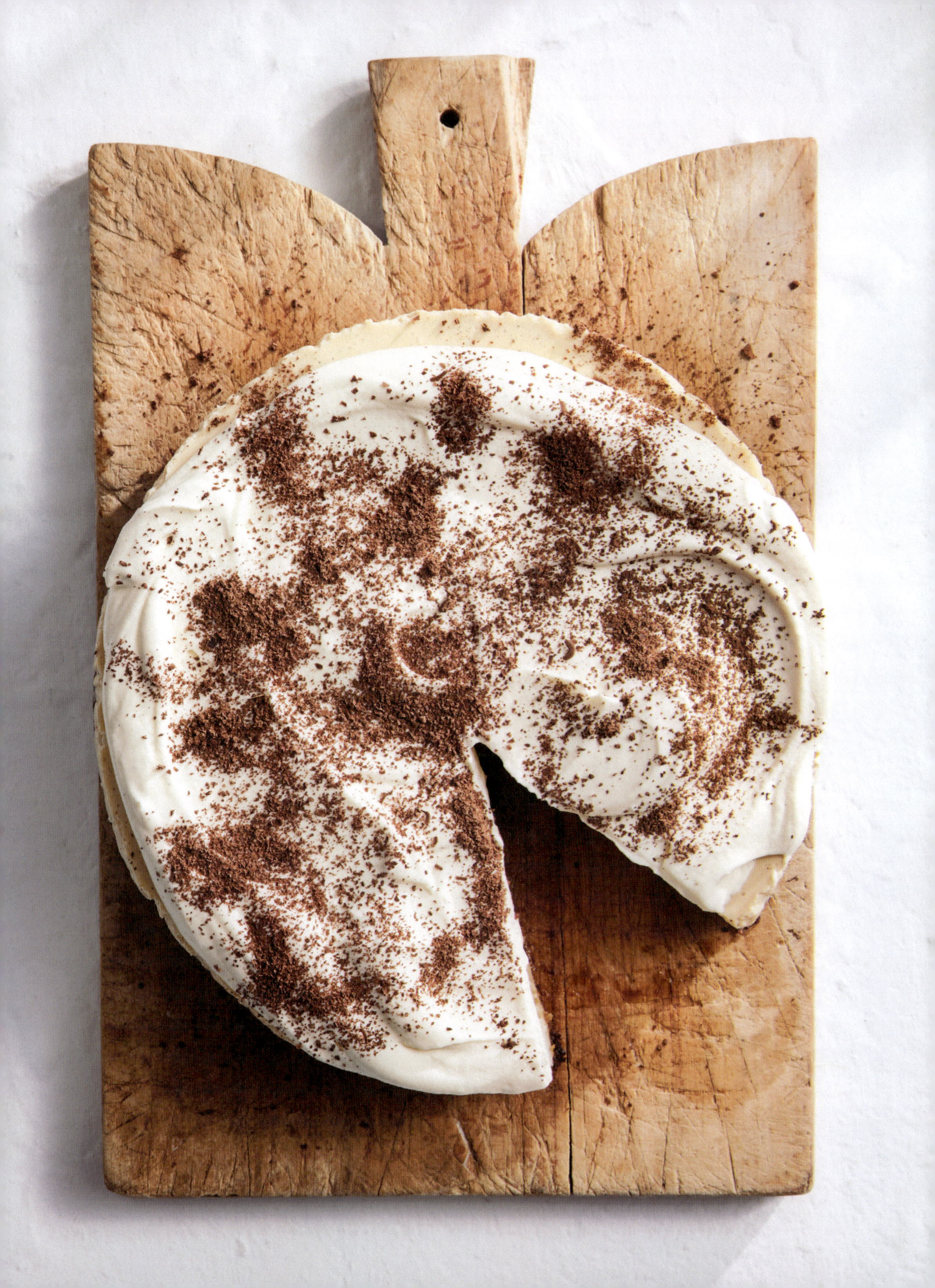

# Late Summer Crumble

*With just-cooked fruit and a crunchy layer of oaty crumble, this is best served with lashings of vanilla bean ice cream. Ring the changes with the berries of your choice.*

**SERVES 4-6**

100 grams butter

1 tablespoon golden syrup

⅔ cup oats

⅔ cup desiccated coconut

⅔ cup plain flour

½ cup brown sugar

6 ripe nectarines, quartered

1 cup raspberries

1 cup blueberries

1 cup blackberries

2 tablespoons caster sugar

**EQUIPMENT:** 24cm ovenproof baking dish.

Preheat the oven to 160°C fan bake.

Melt the butter and golden syrup together in the microwave in a microwave-safe bowl. Put the oats, coconut, flour and brown sugar in a food processor. Add the butter mixture and pulse to combine. Put the fruit into the baking dish and sprinkle over the caster sugar. Squish the crumble mixture into clumps and sprinkle on top of the fruit. Bake for 30 minutes, or until golden.

*dish*.co.nz | DISH 181

# FILL THE TINS

*What could be better than a big pot of tea and a sweet treat as you take a break from the afternoon sun to enjoy a book, crossword or afternoon game of Scrabble? When it comes to baking, we have you covered with some of our all-time favourites – the Sticky Fingers Ginger Loaf with Butterscotch Glaze (page 190) has reached legendary status with dish readers, as has the Take Me With You Cherry Almond and Coconut Slice (page 188), which is perfect for the picnic hamper. The Coconutty Fudge Slice (page 200), with its hit of coconut rum, is strictly for grown-ups, while the kids will be lining up for the Ramp Them Up Blueberry Streusel Muffins (page 186). Filling the tins has never been easier, or more delicious.*

*dish.co.nz* | DISH 183

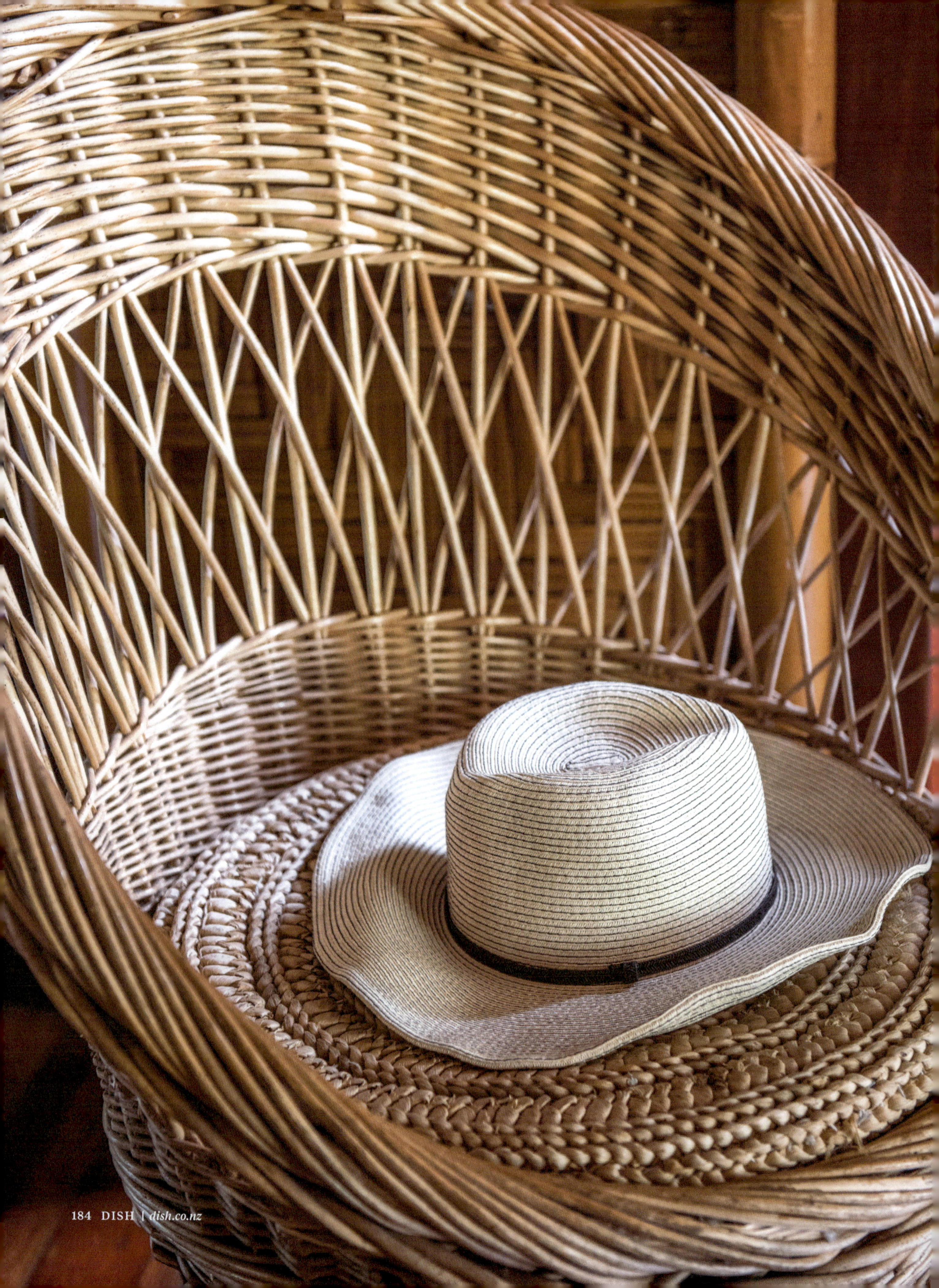

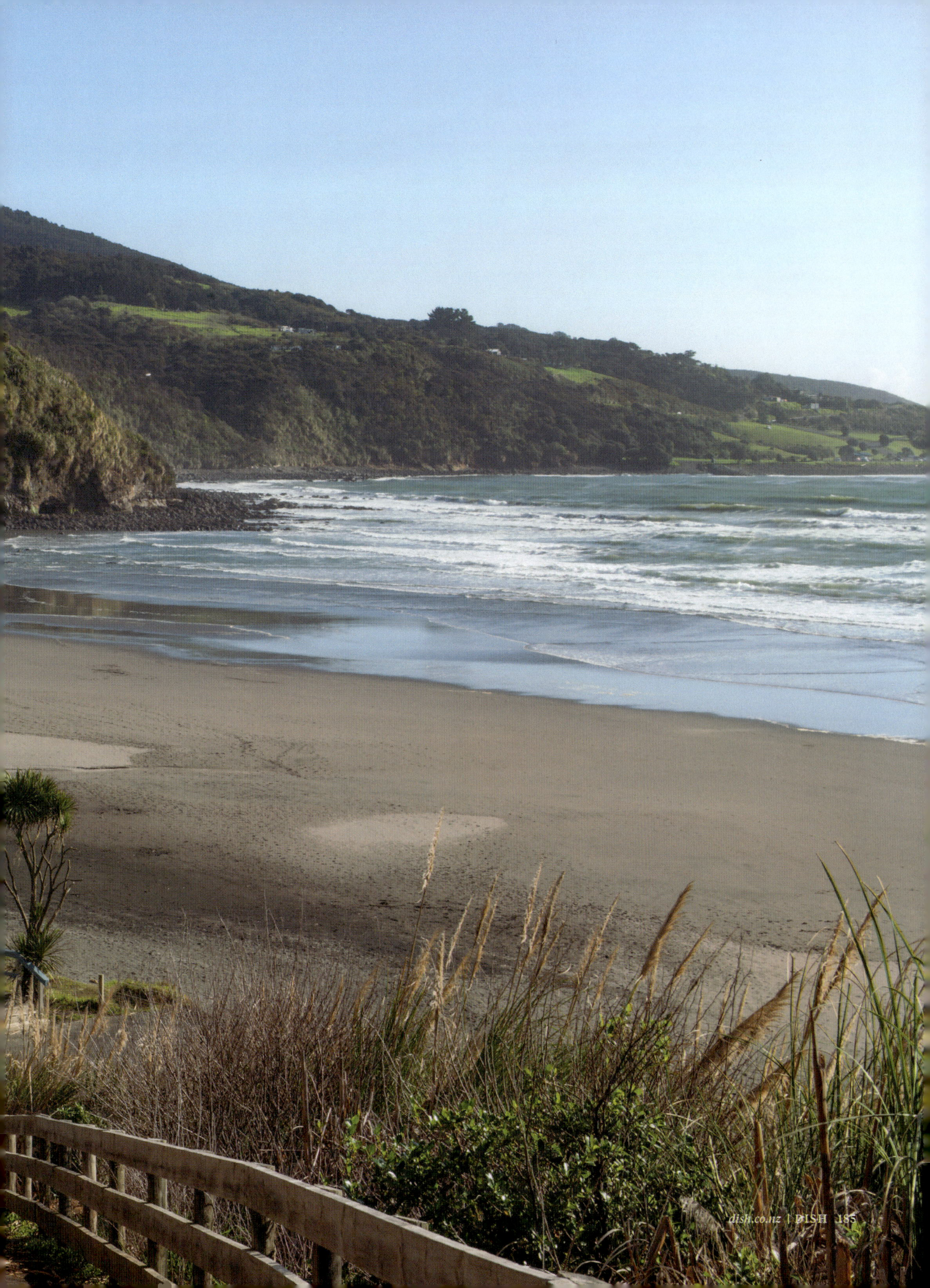

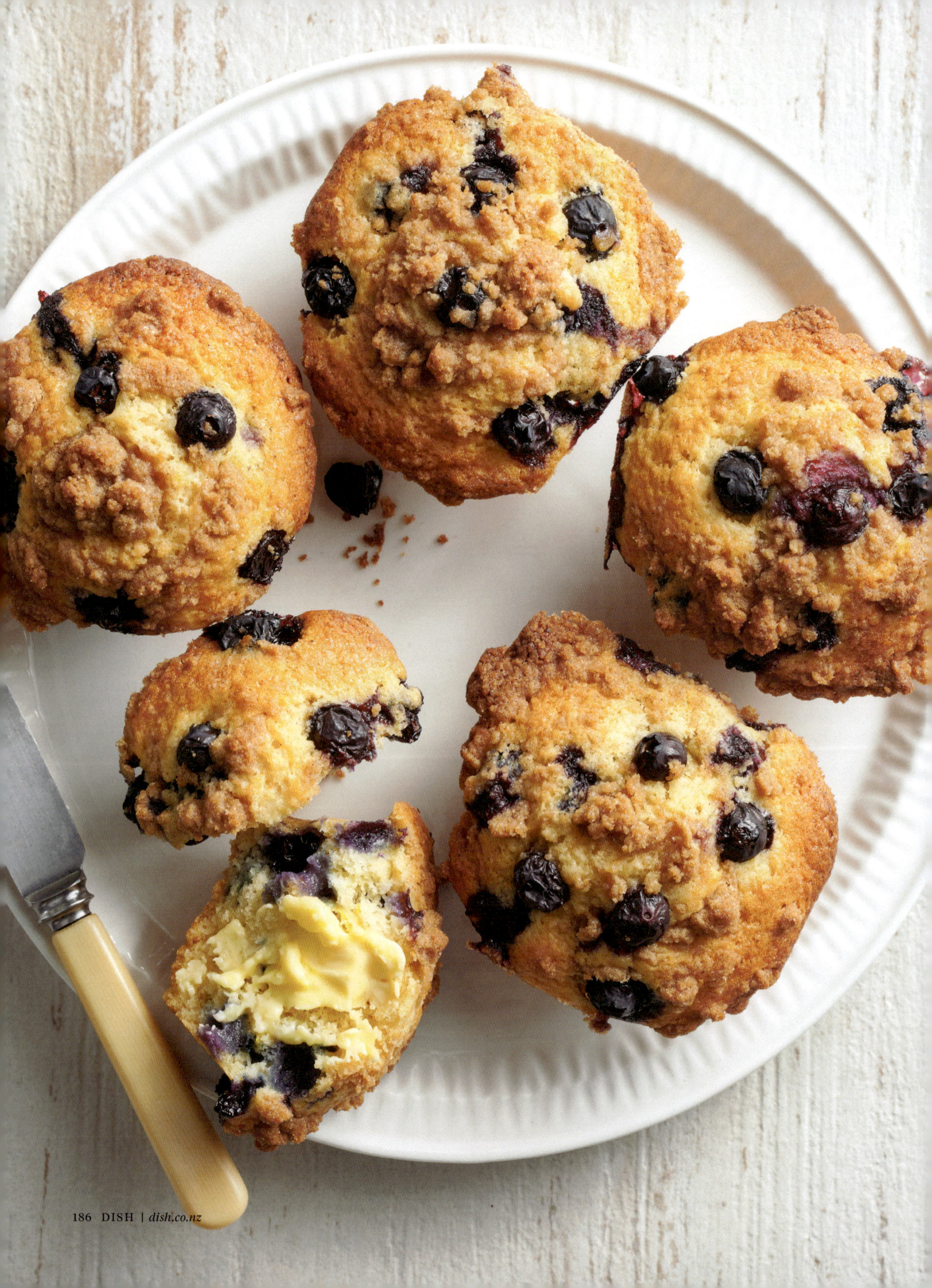

# Ramp Them Up Blueberry Streusel Muffins

*Jam-packed with plump, juicy berries and topped with a lightly spiced streusel, watch these disappear in double-quick time. A slather of good butter is optional but recommended.*

**MAKES 8**

**SPICED STREUSEL**
¼ cup plain flour

¼ cup brown sugar

1 teaspoon ground ginger

½ teaspoon ground cinnamon

45 grams butter, chopped

**MUFFINS**
1⅔ cups plain flour

½ cup caster sugar

2½ teaspoons baking powder

½ teaspoon sea salt

2 cups blueberries

150ml milk

1 large egg

1 teaspoon vanilla extract

⅓ cup rice bran oil

finely grated zest
1 large lemon

**EQUIPMENT:** Grease 8 holes of a standard muffin tray.

Preheat the oven to 160°C fan bake.

**SPICED STREUSEL:** Combine all the ingredients in a bowl. Rub in the butter with your fingertips to make damp, coarse crumbs. Chill until ready to bake.

**MUFFINS:** Mix all the dry ingredients together in a large bowl, then toss through the berries to coat in the flour.

Whisk the milk with the egg, vanilla, oil and lemon zest. Using a large metal spoon, gently fold into the dry ingredients until only just combined. *Don't overmix or the muffins will be tough.*

Spoon the mixture into the tins, then top with the streusel mixture.

Bake for 25 minutes, until puffed and golden on top. *Best eaten on the day of making.*

# Take Me With You Cherry, Almond and Coconut Slice

*With a crisp shortbread base, jammy cherry centre and sticky nutty topping, this is a great holiday picnic treat. Serve with dollops of softly whipped cream for a dessert option.*

**MAKES ABOUT 12 PIECES**

**BASE**

1½ cups plain flour

¾ cup desiccated coconut

½ cup brown sugar

½ teaspoon sea salt

180 grams butter, chopped

**TOPPING**

60 grams butter, chopped

¼ cup caster sugar

2 tablespoons cream

1 teaspoon vanilla extract

150 grams sliced almonds

50 grams thread coconut

**TO ASSEMBLE**

½ cup red berry jam

670-gram jar pitted cherries, well drained and patted dry

**EQUIPMENT:** Grease a 30cm x 21cm slice tin and fully line with baking paper.

Preheat the oven to 170°C regular bake.

**BASE:** Put the flour, coconut, sugar and salt in a food processor and pulse to combine. Add the butter and process until everything is damp and starting to clump together. Tip into the tin and press down firmly to form an even base.

Bake for 15 minutes, until golden and firm. Take out and set aside to cool for 20 minutes.

**TOPPING:** Melt the butter, sugar, cream and vanilla together in a medium saucepan, then stir in the almonds and coconut, turning so everything is well coated.

**TO ASSEMBLE:** Stir the jam and cherries together, then spread evenly over the cooled base. Spoon over the topping.

Bake for about 25 minutes, or until golden and set. Leave to cool in the tin before cutting.

dish.co.nz | DISH 189

# Sticky Fingers Ginger Loaf with Butterscotch Glaze

*Dense, sticky and beautifully spiced, this recipe has been with me since my catering days, which is a very long time ago. Pour the Butterscotch Glaze over the loaf, serve alongside or ditch the glaze and serve plain.*

**MAKES 1 LOAF**

1 cup golden syrup

½ cup water

75 grams butter

½ packed cup brown sugar

finely grated zest 1 orange

1 teaspoon vanilla extract

2 cups plain flour

1 teaspoon each baking soda and ground cinnamon

2 tablespoons ground ginger

½ teaspoon each ground mixed spice and sea salt

¼ cup crystallised ginger, thinly sliced

Butterscotch Glaze (optional, see recipe below)

**EQUIPMENT:** Grease a 5-6 cup-capacity loaf tin and fully line with baking paper.

Preheat the oven to 150°C fan bake.

Put the golden syrup, water, butter, brown sugar, zest and vanilla in a saucepan over a medium-low heat. Stir to melt the sugar and butter, then remove from the heat. Cool for 15 minutes. Sift the flour, baking soda, spices and salt together into a large bowl. Add the cooled syrup mixture and mix until smooth, ensuring there are no pockets of flour in the batter. Pour into the prepared tin and scatter over the sliced ginger. Bake for 35 minutes. Remove from the oven and cover with foil to prevent over-browning. Return to the oven and bake for a further 35 minutes, or until a skewer inserted into the centre comes out clean. Cool in the tin. Drizzle over or serve alongside the glaze, if desired. *The cake is best made a day ahead of eating and keeps beautifully for 4-5 days in an airtight container – add the glaze just before eating.*

# Butterscotch Glaze

**MAKES ½ CUP**

½ packed cup brown sugar

¼ cup cream

1 tablespoon butter

1 teaspoon vanilla extract

Bring all the ingredients to the boil in a small saucepan and simmer for 5 minutes. Cool.

*dish.co.nz* | DISH 191

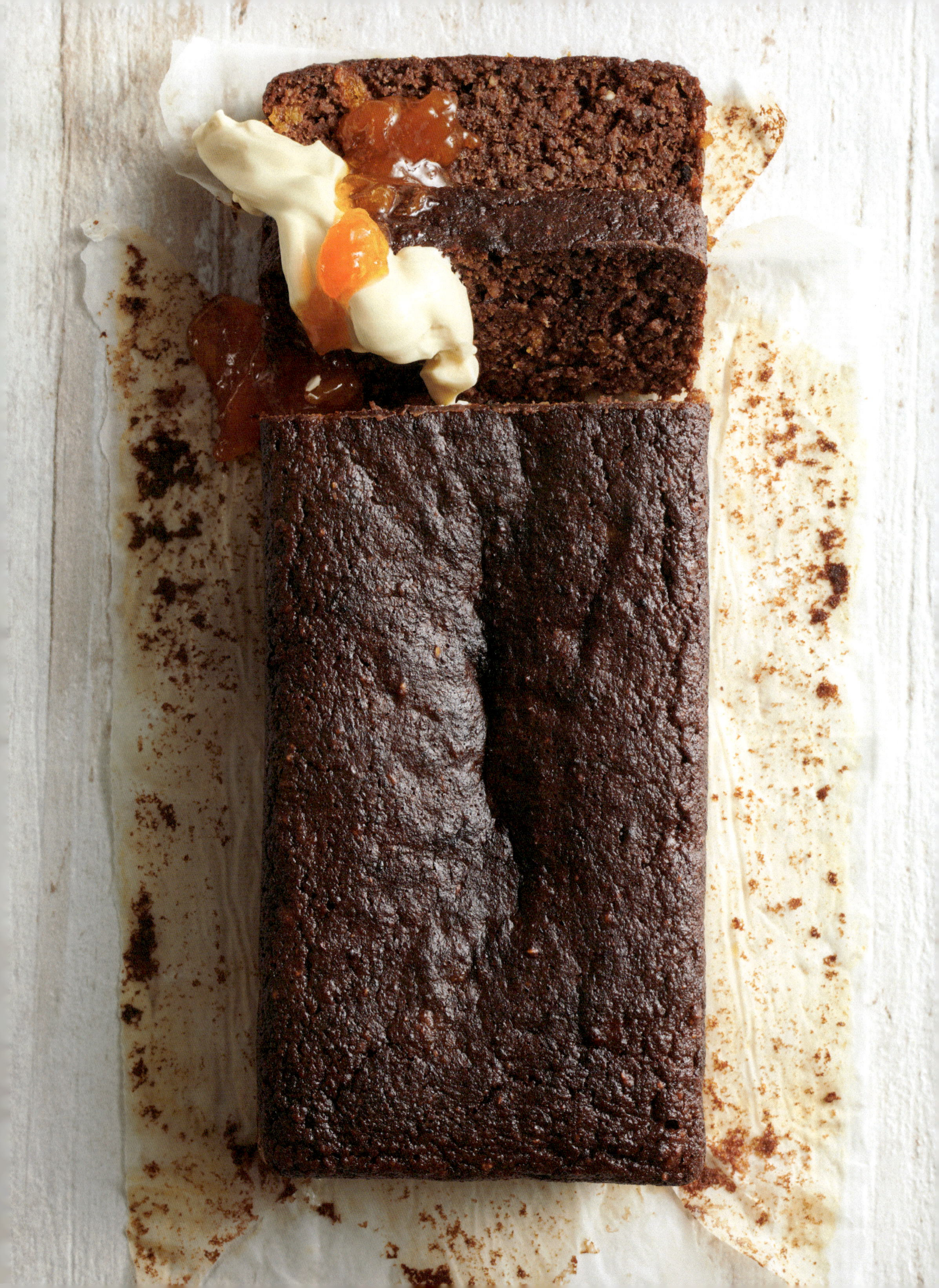

# A Wicked Chocolate and Apricot Loaf (gf)

*Don't let anyone tell you gluten-free is the poor cousin! Cut thick slices of this rich, dense chocolate loaf and wait for the compliments. We served ours with a dollop of clotted cream and apricot jam.*

**MAKES 1 LOAF**

300 grams plump dried apricots, roughly chopped

finely grated zest 1 orange

1½ cups orange juice

1 teaspoon each ground cinnamon and ground ginger

200 grams ground almonds (almond meal)

¾ cup caster sugar

⅓ cup cocoa

1 teaspoon each baking powder and vanilla extract

6 large eggs, lightly whisked

**EQUIPMENT:** Grease a 5-6 cup-capacity loaf tin and fully line with baking paper.

Preheat the oven to 180°C regular bake.

Put the apricots, orange zest, orange juice and spices in a large saucepan and bring to the boil. Cover, reduce the heat to low and simmer for 15-20 minutes, stirring occasionally, until the apricots are very soft and all the liquid has been absorbed. Blitz the mixture with a stick blender to make a thick purée. Set aside to cool.

Add all the remaining ingredients to the cooled apricot paste in the saucepan and stir together until everything is well combined. Pour into the tin, then bake for about 40 minutes, or until a skewer inserted into the centre comes out clean. Cool completely in the tin.

# One-pot Chocolate Cake with Sour Cream and Chocolate Frosting

*Who doesn't love a recipe with only one pot to clean up? This is the perfect cake to sling in the picnic basket or take away for the weekend as the chocolate frosting sets firmly and the cake has a fabulous dense texture.*

**SERVES 8**

75 grams butter

⅓ cup cocoa

⅓ cup rice bran oil

⅔ cup ginger beer

1 cup caster sugar

100 grams dark chocolate, chopped (72% cocoa)

1 large egg

1 teaspoon vanilla extract

1¼ cups plain flour

2 teaspoons baking powder

⅓ cup sour cream

**FROSTING**

150 grams dark chocolate, melted (72% cocoa)

¾ cup sour cream, at room temperature

**EQUIPMENT:** Grease a 20cm springform cake tin and line the base and sides with baking paper.

Preheat the oven to 150°C regular bake.

Put the butter, cocoa, oil and ginger beer in a medium-large saucepan over a medium heat. Bring to the boil, stirring constantly, then take off the heat. Add the sugar and chocolate and stir until smooth and the sugar has melted. Set aside to cool.

Whisk the egg and vanilla into the chocolate mixture until glossy. Fold in the combined flour and baking powder, followed by the sour cream.

Pour into the tin and bake for about 30-35 minutes, or until a skewer inserted into the centre comes out with just a few damp crumbs attached. Leave to cool in the tin, then turn out onto a serving plate.

**FROSTING:** Stir the just warm melted chocolate and sour cream together. Pile on top of the cake and swirl with the back of a spoon.

dish.co.nz | DISH 195

# Chunky Toblerone and Roasted Macadamia Cookies

*If I'm going to eat a cookie, it needs to be a damn delicious one! This ticks all the boxes – just change out the nuts and chocolate for your own favourite combo.*

**MAKES ABOUT 18 COOKIES**

1½ cups plain flour

1 cup rolled oats

½ teaspoon sea salt

½ teaspoon baking soda

250 grams roughly chopped Toblerone

1 cup roasted macadamias, roughly chopped

180 grams butter, melted

1 cup brown sugar

¼ cup caster sugar

2 large eggs

1 teaspoon vanilla extract

**EQUIPMENT:** Grease two flat baking trays and line with baking paper.

Preheat the oven to 180°C regular bake.

Combine the flour, oats, salt, baking soda, Toblerone and macadamias in a large bowl and set aside.

Combine the butter and both sugars in another bowl, then whisk in the eggs and vanilla. Pour into the dry ingredients and stir to combine well.

Scoop out tablespoons of the dough and place on the baking trays about 6cm apart. *Don't overcrowd the trays or they will all melt into one huge cookie.* Lightly flatten with the back of a fork.

Bake in batches for 12-15 minutes, until the cookies are a light golden brown and the outer edges are starting to crisp, but the centres are still a little soft and puffy.

Leave for 5 minutes, then transfer to a cooling rack. The cookies will keep for up to 3 days stored in an airtight container.

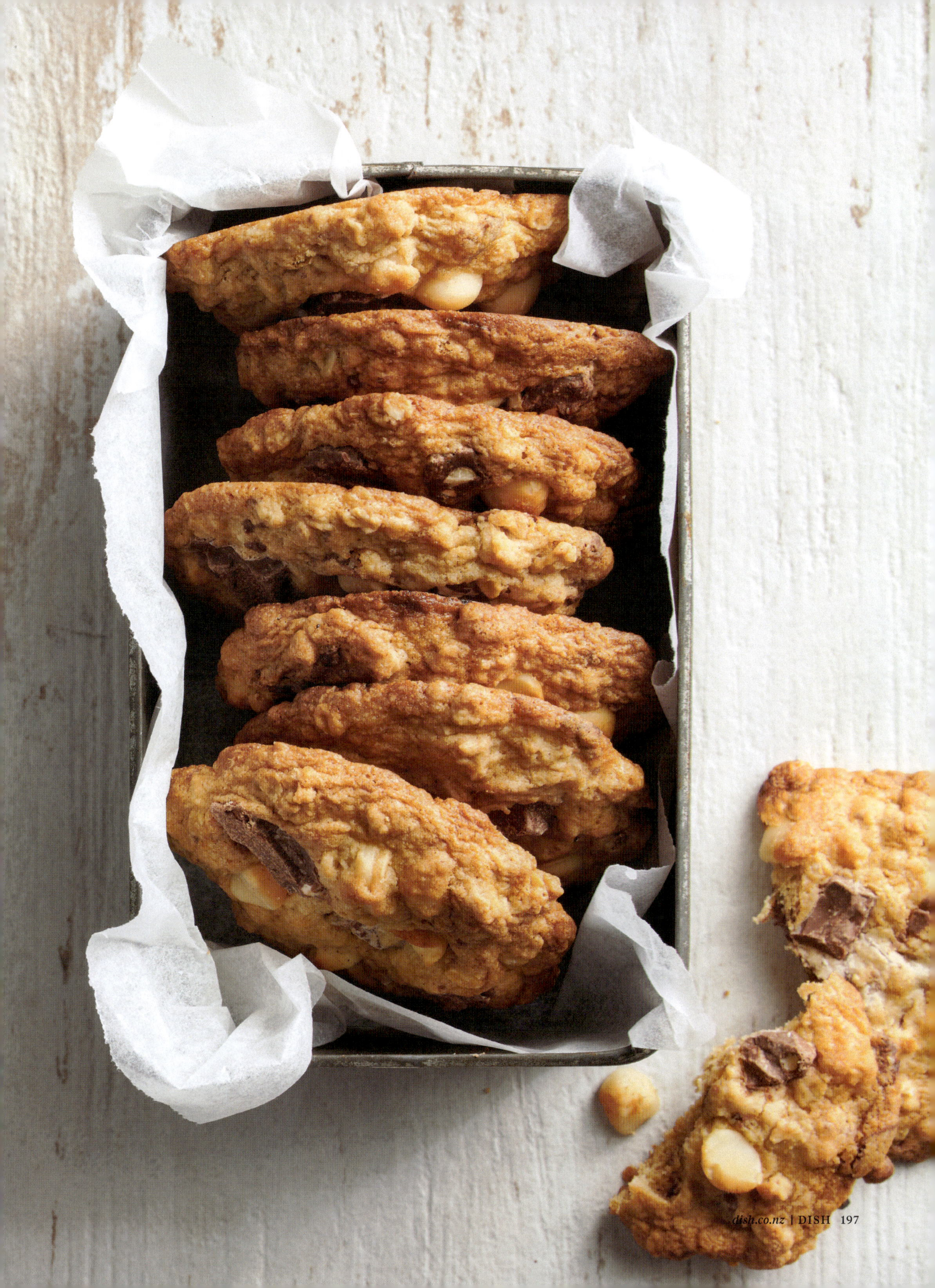

# Coconut Yoghurt Loaf

*Just the ticket to enjoy in a shady spot with a good cup of tea.*

**MAKES 1 LOAF**

2 large eggs

⅔ cup rice bran oil

¾ cup natural yoghurt

finely grated zest 1 lemon

3 tablespoons freshly squeezed lemon juice

¾ cup caster sugar

1 cup desiccated coconut

1½ cups plain flour

2 teaspoons baking powder

**TOPPING**

1½ tablespoons coconut cream

⅓ cup caster sugar

**EQUIPMENT:** Grease a 5-6 cup-capacity loaf tin and fully line with baking paper.

Preheat the oven to 150°C fan bake.

Whisk the eggs, oil, yoghurt, lemon zest, lemon juice and sugar together in a large bowl. Stir in the coconut and sift in the flour and baking powder, then stir to incorporate. Pour into the prepared tin and bake for 45-50 minutes, or until a skewer inserted into the centre comes out clean. Leave to cool for 5 minutes.

**TOPPING:** Whisk together the coconut cream and sugar and pour over the loaf. Leave to cool completely in the tin.

*dish.co.nz* | DISH 199

# Coconutty Fudge Slice

*Strictly for grown-ups, this slice is best eaten later in the evening.*

**MAKES ABOUT 36 PIECES**

190 grams Krispie biscuits

500 grams dark chocolate, roughly chopped

½ cup sweetened condensed milk

¼ cup cream

⅓ cup coconut liqueur (I used coconut rum)

finely grated zest 1 orange

1 cup shredded coconut

⅓ cup finely chopped crystallised ginger

**EQUIPMENT:** Grease a 22cm x 20cm slice tin and fully line with baking paper.

Put the biscuits in a sealed plastic bag and bash with a rolling pin to break into 1-2cm pieces.

Put the chocolate, sweetened condensed milk and cream into a microwave-safe bowl and microwave in 30-second bursts until the chocolate is melted. Whisk in the liqueur until smooth. Fold in the remaining ingredients, reserving a little coconut and ginger. Smooth the mixture into the prepared tin, sprinkle with the reserved coconut and ginger and refrigerate until firm. Slice into small pieces to serve. *Keeps in the fridge for up to 1 week.*

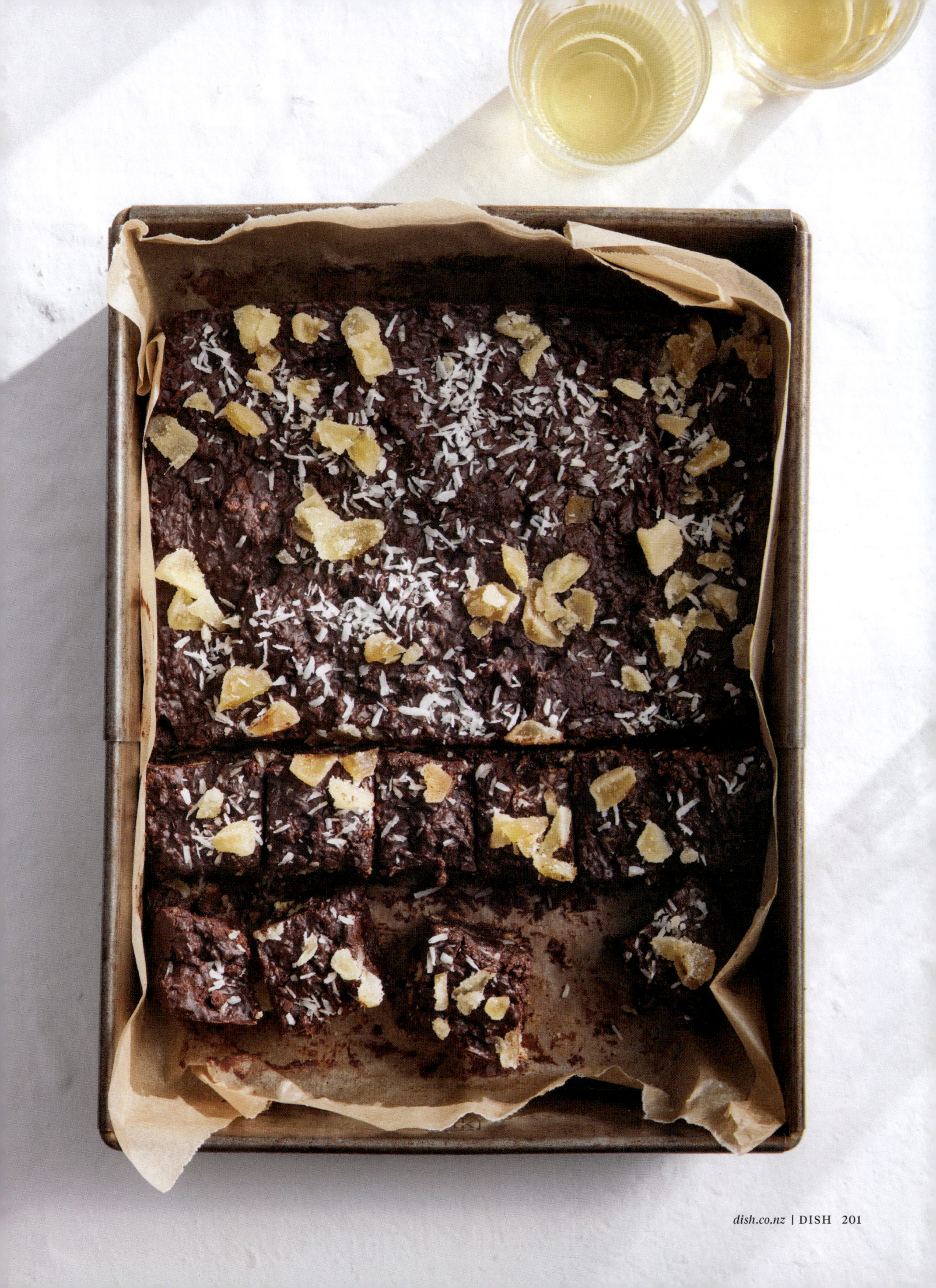

# Oaty Muesli Slice

*This is the perfect bake-and-take slice for a weekend away at the beach.*

**MAKES 15-18 BARS**

1 cup each wholegrain rolled oats, sultanas and roughly chopped walnuts

⅔ cup desiccated coconut

finely grated zest 1 orange

1 cup plain flour

1 teaspoon sea salt

⅔ cup brown sugar

¼ cup golden syrup

125 grams butter

½ teaspoon baking soda

**EQUIPMENT:** Grease a 23cm x 20cm slice tin and fully line with baking paper.

Preheat the oven to 160°C fan bake.

Combine the oats, sultanas, walnuts, coconut, orange zest, flour, salt and sugar in a large mixing bowl. Melt the golden syrup and butter in a small saucepan over a medium heat. Mix the baking soda with 1 tablespoon hot water, then whisk into the melted butter mixture. Add to the dry ingredients and mix well. Press into the prepared tin and bake for 20-25 minutes, or until golden.

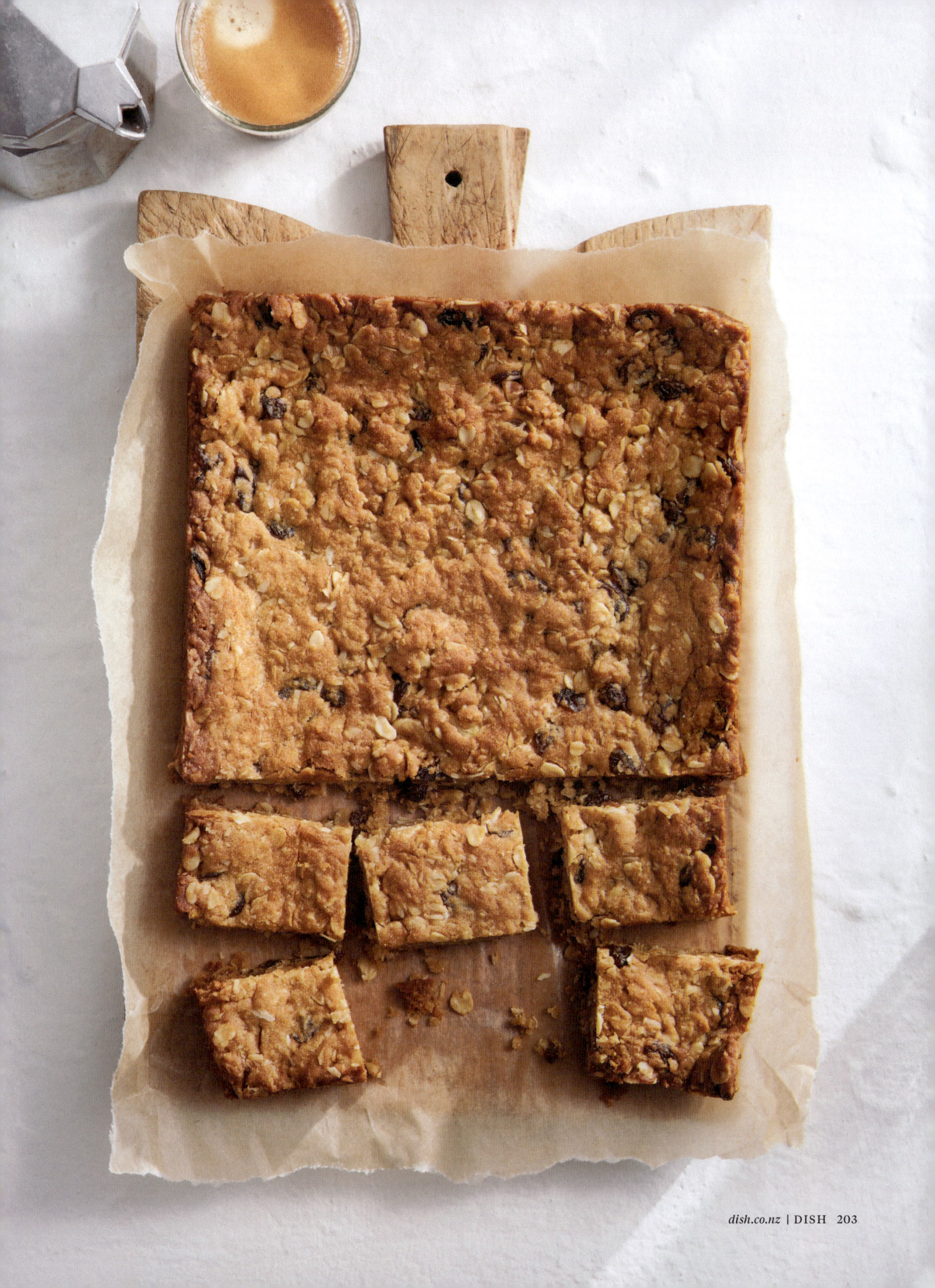

# Claire's Grandmother's Fruit Salad Loaf

*School holidays were always special when spent with my Nana and Poppa. Being a farmer's wife meant Nana always had the tins filled with delicious cakes and slices for the morning and afternoon 'smokos'. This fruit salad loaf was a favourite as it was what Nana called "a great keeper", staying moist right to the last slice.*

**MAKES 1 LOAF**

150 grams butter, softened

175 grams sugar

3 large eggs

175 grams plain flour

pinch of salt

1 teaspoon baking powder

½ teaspoon mixed spice

zest and juice 1 orange

8 plump dried apricots, thinly sliced, plus extra for topping

¼ cup well-drained crushed pineapple

⅓ cup mashed ripe banana

¾ cup icing sugar

zest and juice 1 lemon

**EQUIPMENT:** Grease and line the base and sides of a 5-6 cup-capacity loaf tin with baking paper.

Preheat the oven to 180°C regular bake.

Cream the butter and sugar until pale and creamy. Beat in the eggs one at a time, mixing well each time. Add the combined flour, salt, baking powder and mixed spice, the orange zest and juice and the apricots, pineapple and banana, and fold through with a large metal spoon. Tip into the tin and smooth the top.

Bake for 40-50 minutes, or until firm to the touch and the sides are pulling away from the baking paper. Cool a little before removing from the tin.

Sift the icing sugar into a bowl and add enough lemon juice to make a smooth, pourable icing. Drizzle over the cake, allowing some to run down the sides. Sprinkle over the lemon zest and extra dried apricots while the icing is still wet. The loaf will keep in an airtight container for up to 4 days.

dish.co.nz | DISH 205

# Passionfruit Shortbread

*I've made a lot of shortbread over the years but these remain my favourite. Use passionfruit syrup from the supermarket when the fresh fruit aren't available.*

**MAKES ABOUT 18 DOUBLE BISCUITS**

200 grams butter, at room temperature

1 cup icing sugar

1 teaspoon vanilla extract

2 cups plain flour

¼ cup cornflour

pinch of sea salt

¼ cup passionfruit in syrup, or pulp and seeds of 1-2 large passionfruit

**FILLING**
100 grams butter, at room temperature

1½ cups icing sugar

3 tablespoons passionfruit in syrup, or pulp and seeds of 1-2 large passionfruit

Preheat the oven to 160°C regular bake.

Beat the butter, icing sugar and vanilla until very light and creamy. Sift the flour, cornflour and salt together. Add to the butter mixture along with the passionfruit and beat gently to combine.

Roll tablespoons of the mixture out on a piece of baking paper into logs approximately 6cm long x 1.5cm wide. Place on a lined baking tray and refrigerate until firm.

Bake for 18-20 minutes, until lightly golden. Leave on the tray for 5 minutes, then carefully transfer to a cooling rack.

**FILLING:** Beat the butter and icing sugar until creamy, then beat in the passionfruit. Transfer to a piping bag with a fluted nozzle. Pipe a line of filling on half of the biscuits, then sandwich with the remaining biscuits. Dust with icing sugar to serve.

*dish.co.nz* | DISH 207

# SAUCY BITS

*To put a little extra somethin' somethin' into any meal, may we present our fabulous range of sauces, mayos, dressings and toppings – guaranteed to elevate every occasion!*

# American Ranch Mayo (gf) (v)

*Enjoy with chicken wings, pork spare ribs, burgers, vegetables for dipping, fried chicken, tacos, potato salad or egg sandwiches.*

**MAKES ABOUT 1¼ CUPS**

100 grams soft blue cheese

2 cloves garlic, crushed

2 tablespoons sour cream

1 teaspoon lemon juice

1 teaspoon sea salt

2 teaspoons finely chopped parsley

¾ cup good-quality egg mayonnaise

Put the blue cheese and garlic on a plate and mash together with a fork. Stir in all the remaining ingredients.

# Beer and Hoisin-braised Onions (v)

*Use a rich, smoky but not bitter beer that will work with the hoisin to give the onions a great barbecue sauce flavour.*

**MAKES ABOUT 2 CUPS**

2 tablespoons vegetable oil

small knob butter

4 large brown onions, peeled and sliced

sea salt

2 tablespoons brown sugar

2 cloves garlic, crushed

¼ cup hoisin sauce

½ cup dark beer

1 tablespoon tomato paste

1 tablespoon soy sauce

¼ teaspoon dried chilli flakes

Heat the oil and butter in a large frying pan and add the onions with a good pinch of salt. Cook for 10 minutes, then stir in the brown sugar. Whisk the garlic, hoisin, beer, tomato paste, soy sauce and chilli flakes together in a bowl and add to the onions. Cook gently for about 15 minutes, stirring occasionally, until reduced and glossy.

# Caramelised Onions (gf) (v)

*Caramelised onions are quick and easy to make, enhance all kinds of dishes and keep in a sealed container in the fridge for up to a week.*

**MAKES ABOUT 1½ CUPS**

1 tablespoon olive oil

1 tablespoon butter

4 large brown onions, sliced

2 cloves garlic, crushed

sea salt and ground pepper

2 tablespoons balsamic glaze

1 tablespoon brown sugar

Heat the oil and butter in a large frying pan and add the onions and garlic. Season generously and cook for 20 minutes, stirring occasionally, until soft. Increase the heat and add the balsamic glaze and brown sugar.

Cook until the onions are sticky and well glazed, about 20 minutes. Cool before using.

# Curried Mango Chutney Mayo (gf) (v)

*Enjoy with potato salad, burgers, fish and chips, vege fritters or chicken sandwiches.*

**MAKES ABOUT 1 CUP**

2 teaspoons mild curry powder

¾ cup good-quality egg mayonnaise

2 tablespoons mango chutney, mild or hot according to taste

1 teaspoon each lemon juice and sea salt

Warm the curry powder in a dry frying pan over a low heat until it smells fragrant and turns a slightly darker colour. Don't let it burn. Stir into the mayo along with the chutney, lemon juice and salt.

# Herb and Pistachio Dressing (gf) (v)

*Bright with the flavours of basil, lemon and pistachio, this fragrant dressing is great with all barbecued meats.*

**MAKES ABOUT ½ CUP**

¼ cup shelled pistachios

¼ cup each packed basil and mint

2 cloves garlic, crushed

2 tablespoons lemon juice

1 teaspoon sea salt

2 teaspoons runny honey

⅓ cup olive oil

Place all the ingredients in a small food processor and process until smooth.

# Herby Yoghurt Mayo (gf) (v)

*This light and zesty mayo is a perfect foil for the richness of salmon.*

**MAKES ABOUT 1¾ CUPS**

1 cup natural Greek yoghurt

½ cup good-quality egg mayonnaise

1 tablespoon lemon juice

3 tablespoons roughly chopped capers, plus 1 tablespoon whole to garnish

3 tablespoons chopped fresh dill, plus a few fronds to garnish

3 tablespoons chopped fresh mint

sea salt and ground pepper

Mix the yoghurt, mayonnaise and lemon juice in a small bowl. Add the chopped capers, dill and mint, and season to taste. *For a little extra drama, a drizzle of pomegranate molasses swirled through the mayo is also a tasty option.* Cover and refrigerate until ready to serve.

# Honey-roasted Apricots (gf)

*Delicious on cakes, to top tarts, on your breakfast yoghurt – or straight from the baking dish.*

**MAKES ABOUT 2 CUPS**

12 firm but ripe apricots

⅓ cup honey

⅓ cup white wine

1 teaspoon vanilla paste or extract

¼ teaspoon ground pepper

Preheat the oven to 180°C fan bake.

Combine the apricots, honey, wine, vanilla and pepper in a shallow baking dish. Roast the apricots for 10-12 minutes, basting once until soft but not falling apart. Set aside to cool.

# Lemon, Tarragon and Mustard Mayo (gf) (v)

*Enjoy with chicken sandwiches and salads, fish, lamb, beef, pork terrine, pork belly, potato salads and burgers.*

**MAKES JUST UNDER 1 CUP**

1 tablespoon wholegrain mustard

1½ teaspoons dried tarragon

2 cloves garlic, crushed

finely grated zest 1 lemon

1 teaspoon sea salt

¾ cup good-quality egg mayonnaise

Add all the ingredients to the mayonnaise and stir to combine.

# Miso and Sesame Mayo (v)

*Enjoy with fries and tempura, sushi, roast pork or chicken salads, grilled eggplant, karaage chicken or egg salad.*

**MAKES JUST UNDER 1 CUP**

2 tablespoons white miso paste

¾ cup good-quality egg mayonnaise

2 teaspoons sesame oil

1 teaspoon tamari

1 teaspoon white sesame seeds, toasted

Stir the miso paste and 2 tablespoons mayonnaise together until smooth. Stir in the sesame oil and tamari, then add to the remaining mayo and combine. Scatter over the sesame seeds.

# Pineapple Sambal

*Fresh and sweet, this irresistible sambal is great alongside roast pork or ham, or to top tacos.*

**MAKES 2 CUPS**

½ small telegraph cucumber, peeled, seeded and finely diced

1 cup finely chopped fresh pineapple

1 long red chilli, seeded and finely chopped

1 shallot, very thinly sliced

2 teaspoons fish sauce

2 teaspoons caster sugar

2 tablespoons lime juice

Combine all the ingredients in a bowl.

# Pizza Dough (v)

*I use instant dried yeast that comes packaged in single-use foil sachets and is available in the baking section at supermarkets. The yeast is added to the dry ingredients as described and is not activated in warm liquid first. The water measurement in a dough recipe is only a guide and you may need to add more depending on the dryness of the flour, or add more flour if the dough is too wet.*

**MAKES 2 PIZZA BASES**

2 cups high-grade flour

1½ teaspoons instant dried yeast

1½ teaspoons sea salt

1 teaspoon caster sugar

225ml warm water

1 tablespoon olive oil

Combine the flour, yeast, salt and sugar in a large bowl. Tip in the combined water and oil and bring together to make a soft shaggy dough. Tip onto a lightly floured bench and bring together with your hands. Knead for 5 minutes until smooth and elastic.

Place in a large, oiled bowl and turn the dough to lightly coat in the oil. Cover with plastic wrap. Set aside in a draught-free place for 1½-2 hours to double in size.

When the dough has risen, remove from the bowl and divide in half.

Dust with flour then place on a sheet of baking paper and roll out or flatten the dough with your fingers to the desired shape.

**COOK'S NOTE:** This dough can be made 2 days ahead of using. If making ahead, cover and refrigerate after the initial kneading or divide between 2 large sealable plastic bags. Use straight from the fridge when ready to assemble and cook. If only making 1 pizza, freeze the other half of the dough in a plastic bag for another day.

# Salsa Verde Mayo (gf)

*Enjoy with fish cakes, fish burgers, roasted vege salads, barbecued lamb, grilled chicken or salmon.*

**MAKES ABOUT 1¼ CUPS**

½ cup herbs, use any combination of parsley, mint, basil, oregano and dill

3 anchovy fillets

2 cloves garlic, crushed

1 tablespoon capers

¾ cup good-quality egg mayonnaise

finely grated zest 1 lemon

1 teaspoon each lemon juice and sea salt

Put the herbs, anchovies, garlic and capers on a chopping board and chop everything together. Add to the mayo along with the lemon zest and juice and the salt and stir to combine.

# Salted Caramel Sauce (gf)

*Everyone needs a good caramel sauce in their repertoire!*

**MAKES ABOUT 1½ CUPS**

1½ cups caster sugar

⅓ cup water

1¼ cups cream, warm

2 tablespoons butter

1 heaped teaspoon sea salt

Place the caster sugar and water in a medium saucepan and whisk to combine. Bring to a simmer, whisking to dissolve the sugar, then stop stirring.

Continue heating the sugar mixture, using a small pastry brush to brush down any excess sugar from the sides of the pot, until the sugar first becomes white and crystallised, then starts to turn a light amber. To combine the sugar and encourage even caramelisation, give the pot a gentle swirl.

As soon as it is a good golden colour, remove the saucepan from the heat and whisk in the cream. It will froth up madly but keep whisking and it will settle down. Add the butter and sea salt and whisk until smooth. Pour into a jar, cool and store in the fridge for up to two weeks. Reheat briefly to serve.

# Satay Sauce (v)

*Great with beef, chicken, lamb and vegetables.
You can add a pinch of chilli flakes for a spicy version.*

**MAKES ABOUT 1½ CUPS**

¾ cup coconut cream

¼ cup water

½ cup crunchy or smooth peanut butter

1 tablespoon soy sauce

2 cloves garlic, crushed

2 teaspoons brown sugar

1 teaspoon each sesame oil and sea salt

2 teaspoons lime juice

Place all the ingredients in a saucepan and simmer for 5 minutes. Cool and keep in a sealed container in the fridge for up to 5 days.

# Soy and Lime Dipping Sauce (v)

*This sauce sings with pork, but is also great with dumplings or sashimi.*

**MAKES ⅓ CUPS**

2 tablespoons each soy sauce, kecap manis and black vinegar

½ teaspoon grated fresh ginger

2 teaspoons lime juice

1-2 teaspoons chilli sauce, e.g., sriracha

1 clove garlic, crushed

Combine all the ingredients in a bowl.

# Smoky Paprika and Sherry Vinegar Mayo (gf) (v)

*Enjoy with paella, roast potatoes, vege salads, clams and mussels, croquettas, meatballs or arancini.*

**MAKES JUST UNDER 1 CUP**

1 teaspoon smoked paprika

2 cloves garlic, crushed

2 teaspoons sherry vinegar

1 teaspoon sea salt

¾ cup good-quality egg mayonnaise

Add all the ingredients to the mayonnaise and stir to combine.

# Tartare Sauce (gf) (v)

*An all-time classic sauce for fish or other seafood.*

**MAKES ABOUT ¾ CUP**

½ cup good-quality egg mayonnaise

2 tablespoons finely chopped gherkins

1 tablespoon grain mustard

1 tablespoon chopped capers

finely grated zest 1 lemon

1 tablespoon lemon juice

1 teaspoon dried tarragon

2 cloves garlic, crushed

1 teaspoon sea salt

Combine all the ingredients in a bowl.

# Tomato, Capsicum and Chilli Relish

*Use on burgers, in toasties and alongside barbecued meats or veg. It's also delicious with cheese. Cinnamon, star anise and a dash of fish sauce add a fabulous depth of flavour.*

**MAKES 2 CUPS**

2 tablespoons vegetable oil

1 brown onion, thinly sliced

1 red capsicum, seeded and thinly sliced

2 cloves garlic, crushed

1 teaspoon sea salt

1 tablespoon grated fresh ginger

1 small cinnamon stick

1 whole star anise

1 teaspoon fish sauce

¾ cup caster sugar

½ cup cider vinegar or white wine vinegar

500 grams ripe tomatoes, roughly chopped

3 long red chillies, halved, seeded and roughly chopped

Heat the oil in a large saucepan and add the onion, capsicum, garlic, salt, ginger, cinnamon stick and star anise. Cover and cook over a medium low heat for 10 minutes until the vegetables are tender, stirring occasionally so it doesn't catch on the base of the pan. Add the fish sauce and sugar and cook for 2 minutes, stirring until lightly caramelised. Add all the remaining ingredients. Bring to the boil, then reduce the heat to low and cook very gently for about 1 hour, stirring occasionally until well-reduced, thick and glossy. Cool, then store in a sealed container in the fridge for up to 1 week.

# Walnut Praline (gf)

*Double the nuts and add 1 teaspoon sea salt to make an amazing snack to nibble over drinks.*

**MAKES ENOUGH TO TOP 1 TART, PLUS EXTRAS TO SNACK ON**

⅔ cup caster sugar

1 tablespoon water

1 cup walnut halves

Put the caster sugar and water together in a pan and whisk to start the sugar dissolving. Cook, without stirring, over a medium heat until the mixture has crystallised, then turned a transparent light golden colour. As soon as you have an amber liquid, add the walnuts, swirl to coat, then pour them onto your lined oven tray, making loose patterns if desired. Leave to set, then smash into chunks with the end of a rolling pin or use in whole pieces.

# Conversions

**OVEN TEMPERATURES**

| Celsius | Fahrenheit | Gas number | Oven terms |
| --- | --- | --- | --- |
| 110°C | 225°F | ¼ | Very cool |
| 130°C | 250°F | ½ | Very slow |
| 140°C | 275°F | 1 | Very slow |
| 150°C | 300°F | 2 | Slow |
| 165°C | 325°F | 3 | Slow |
| 177°C | 350°F | 4 | Moderate |
| 190°C | 375°F | 5 | Moderate |
| 200°C | 400°F | 6 | Moderately hot |
| 220°C | 425°F | 9 | Hot |
| 230°C | 450°F | 9 | Hot |
| 245°C | 475°F | 10 | Hot |
| 260°C | 500°F | 10 | Extremely hot |
| 290°C | 550°F | 10 | Grill/broil |

**BUTTER CONVERSION**

| 50 grams | 1¾ ounces | 3½ tablespoons |
| 100 grams | 3½ ounces | 7 tablespoons |
| 110 grams | 4 ounces | 1 stick |
| 125 grams | 4½ ounces | 9 tablespoons |
| 150 grams | 5 ounces | 10½ tablespoons |
| 200 grams | 7 ounces | 1¾ sticks |
| 250 grams | 9 ounces | 1 cup |

**WEIGHT**

| Metric | Imperial |
| --- | --- |
| 10 grams | ¼ ounces |
| 15 grams | ½ ounces |
| 25 grams | ¾ ounces |
| 60 grams | 2 ounces |
| 125 grams | 4 ounces |
| 180 grams | 6 ounces |
| 250 grams | 8 ounces |
| 500 grams | 16 ounces (1 pound) |
| 1 kilogram | 32 ounces (2 pounds) |

**VOLUME MEASURES**

| Cup | Metric | Imperial |
| --- | --- | --- |
| ¼ cup | 60 ml | 2 fl oz |
| ⅓ cup | 80 ml | 2½ fl oz |
| ½ cup | 125 ml | 4 fl oz |
| ⅔ cup | 160 ml | 5 fl oz |
| ¾ cup | 180 ml | 6 fl oz |
| 1 cup | 250 ml | 8 fl oz |
| 2 cups | 500 ml | 16 fl oz (1 American pint) |
| 2½ cups | 600 ml | 20 fl oz (1 imperial pint) |
| 4 cups | 1 litre | 32 fl oz |

**FURTHER VOLUME MEASURES**

1 teaspoon = 5 ml

1 North American, New Zealand and United Kingdom tablespoon = 15 ml

1 Australian tablespoon = 20 ml

| Volume | Metric | Imperial |
| --- | --- | --- |
| ¼ teaspoon | 1.25 ml | |
| ½ teaspoon | 2.5 ml | |
| 1 teaspoon | 5 ml | |
| ½ cup | 125 ml | 4 fl oz |
| 1 cup liquid | 250 ml | 8 fl oz |
| 1 (American) pint | 500 ml | 16 fl oz |
| 1 litre | 1000 ml | 32 fl oz |

**DIMENSIONS**

Dimensions 1 inch = 2.5 cm

1 cup (volume) = 250 ml

**LENGTH**

| Centimetres | Inches |
| --- | --- |
| 1 cm | ½ inch |
| 2.5 cm | 1 inch |
| 12 cm | 4½ inches |
| 20 cm | 8 inches |
| 24 cm | 9½ inches |
| 30 cm | 12 inches |

**INGREDIENT EQUIVALENTS**

| American mustard | Yellow mustard |
|---|---|
| Baking soda | Bicarbonate of soda |
| Beetroot | Beets |
| Biscuits | Cookies |
| Broad beans | Fava beans |
| Capsicum | Bell pepper |
| Caster sugar | Superfine sugar |
| Celeriac | Celery root |
| Chickpeas | Garbanzo beans |
| Coriander | Cilantro |
| Cornflour | Cornstarch |
| Cos lettuce | Romaine lettuce |
| Dried red chilli | Red pepper |
| Eggplant | Aubergine |
| Grill | Broil |
| Ground almonds | Almond meal |
| Gai larn | Chinese broccoli |
| Icing sugar | Confectioner's sugar |
| Kūmara | Sweet potato |
| Mince | Ground meat |
| Plain flour | All-purpose flour |
| Pumpkin | Squash |
| Prawns | Shrimp |
| Rocket | Arugula |
| Scone | Biscuits |
| Snow peas | Mange tout |
| Stock cubes | Bouillon cubes |
| Spring onion | Scallion |
| White sugar | Granulated sugar |
| Zucchini | Courgette |

# Index

## A

American Ranch Mayo (gf) (v) — **210**

Aromatic Peppercorn Chicken with Hot and Sweet Dipping Sauce (gf) — **94**

**APRICOTS – SEE STONE FRUIT**

**ASPARAGUS**

Crisp Lettuce and Asparagus Salad with Tarragon Aioli and Soft Eggs (gf) — **130**

**AVOCADO**

Avocado, Broad Bean and Goat's Cheese Salad (gf) (v) — **132**

Sausage Coil with Charred Broccolini and Avocado and Olive Salsa (gf) — **74**

Spice-roasted Carrot and Avocado Salad (gf) (v) — **116**

Whipped Avocado with Silken Tofu, Lime and Jalapeño (gf) (v) — **10**

*Avocado, Broad Bean and Goat's Cheese Salad (gf) (v)* — **132**

## B

**BACON**

Crispy Chicken and Bacon Burgers — **142**

Lamb and Bacon-wrapped Date Kebabs (gf) — **76**

*Baked Prawns with Lemon and Feta (gf)* — **56**

*Baked Spanish Rice with Chicken and Chorizo (gf)* — **62**

*Baked Tomatoes and Spaghetti (v)* — **50**

*Barbecued Butterflied Leg of Lamb with Herb and Parmesan Dressing (gf)* — **96**

*Barbecued Pork, Mango and Herb Salad* — **112**

**BEANS**

Avocado, Broad Bean and Goat's Cheese Salad (gf) (v) — **132**

Two-bean and Crisp Flatbread Salad with Soft Eggs (v) — **106**

**BEEF**

Beef Short Ribs — **90**

Beef and Smoked Cheddar Burgers — **148**

Grilled Steak Sandwich with Caramelised Onions and Mushrooms — **84**

Reuben Sliders — **30**

Steak Tacos with Charred Pineapple Salsa — **82**

*Beef Short Ribs* — **90**

*Beef and Smoked Cheddar Burgers* — **148**

*Beer Can Chicken with White Barbecue Sauce* — **88**

*Beer and Hoisin-braised Onions (v)* — **210**

**BEETROOT**

Roasted Beetroot, Blue Cheese
and Pistachio Salad (gf) (v)    126

**BERRIES**

Late Summer Crumble    180

Lemon Meringue and Blueberry
Pie Ice Cream    162

Ramp Them Up Blueberry Streusel
Muffins    186

Rhubarb and Strawberry
Frangipane Tarts    168

*Best-ever Fresh Catch
Beer-battered Fish*    60

**BISCUITS – SEE COOKIES**

**BLUE CHEESE**

Blue Cheese Mayo (gf) (v)    142

Roasted Beetroot, Blue Cheese
and Pistachio Salad (gf) (v)    126

*Blue Cheese Mayo (gf) (v)*    142

**BLUEBERRIES – SEE BERRIES**

*Boozy Barbecued Stone Fruit
Parcels*    164

**BURGERS**

Beef and Smoked Cheddar Burgers    148

Chorizo and Garlic Prawn Burgers    144

Crispy Chicken and Bacon Burgers    142

Crispy Spiced Onion Fritter Burgers
with Mango Chutney (v)    140

Kiwi Lamb Burgers    138

Moroccan Lamb Burgers, Grilled
Haloumi and Pistachio Salsa    146

*Butterscotch Glaze (gf)*    190

# C

**CABBAGE**

Seeded Slaw (gf) (v)    104

*Cacio e Pepe Pizza (v)*    40

**CAKES**

Claire's Grandmother's Fruit
Salad Loaf    204

Coconut Yoghurt Loaf    198

Olive Oil and Orange Cake with
Honey-roasted Apricots    158

One-pot Chocolate Cake with Sour
Cream and Chocolate Frosting    194

Sticky Fingers Ginger Loaf with
Butterscotch Glaze    190

A Wicked Chocolate and
Apricot Loaf (gf)    192

**CARAMEL**

Macadamia Caramel Tart    176

Salted Caramel Sauce (gf)    216

*Caramelised Onions (gf) (v)*    211

**CARROTS**

Spice-roasted Carrot and Avocado

Salad (gf) (v)   **116**

**CHEESE – SEE ALSO BLUE CHEESE, FETA, GOAT'S CHEESE, HALOUMI, MOZZARELLA AND RICOTTA**

Beef and Smoked Cheddar Burgers   **148**

Cacio e Pepe Pizza (v)   **40**

**CHEESECAKE**

Spiced Pumpkin Cheesecake Tart   **170**

Tiramisu Espresso Martini No-bake Cheesecake   **178**

**CHERRIES**

Take Me With You Cherry, Almond and Coconut Slice   **188**

**CHICKEN**

Aromatic Peppercorn Chicken with Hot and Sweet Dipping Sauce (gf)   **94**

Baked Spanish Rice with Chicken and Chorizo (gf)   **62**

Beer Can Chicken with White Barbecue Sauce   **88**

Chicken Katsu Sliders   **14**

Chicken with Yoghurt, Caramelised Onions and Cashew Nuts (gf)   **98**

Crispy Chicken and Bacon Burgers   **142**

Lemony Sumac Chicken and Chickpea Salad with Dates, Feta and Baby Spinach   **110**

Smoked Chicken and Mango Salad with Crispy Noodles and Peanut

Dressing   **122**

*Chicken Katsu Sliders*   **14**

*Chicken with Yoghurt, Caramelised Onions and Cashew Nuts (gf)*   **98**

**CHICKPEAS**

Lemony Sumac Chicken and Chickpea Salad with Dates, Feta and Baby Spinach   **110**

*Chilled Espresso Martini Affogato (gf)*   **156**

*Chilli Prawn Pasta*   **52**

*Chipotle Prawns with Lime and Jalapeño Mayo (gf)*   **80**

*Chips (gf) (v)*   **60**

**CHOCOLATE**

Chunky Toblerone and Roasted Macadamia Cookies   **196**

Coconutty Fudge Slice   **200**

Double Chocolate, Roasted Peanut and Tahini Skillet Cookie (gf)   **174**

One-pot Chocolate Cake with Sour Cream and Chocolate Frosting   **194**

A Wicked Chocolate and Apricot Loaf (gf)   **192**

**CHORIZO**

Baked Spanish Rice with Chicken and Chorizo (gf)   **62**

Chorizo and Garlic Prawn Burgers   **144**

Prawn and Chorizo Kebabs with
Smoked Paprika Mayo (gf) **12**

*Chorizo and Garlic Prawn Burgers* **144**

*Christmas Champagne Cocktail* **32**

*Chunky Toblerone and Roasted Macadamia Cookies* **196**

*Claire's Grandmother's Fruit Salad Loaf* **204**

*Classic Lemon Tart* **172**

## COCONUT

Coconut Yoghurt Loaf **198**

Coconutty Fudge Slice **200**

Take Me With You Cherry, Almond and Coconut Slice **188**

*Coconut Yoghurt Loaf* **198**

*Coconutty Fudge Slice* **200**

## CONDIMENTS

American Ranch Mayo (gf) (v) **210**

Avocado and Jalapeño Sauce (gf) (v) **24**

Blue Cheese Mayo (gf) (v) **142**

Charred Pineapple Salsa (gf) (v) **82**

Curried Mango Chutney Mayo (gf) (v) **211**

Green Olive, Jalapeño and Tomato Salsa (gf) (v) **54**

Herb and Parmesan Dressing (gf) (v) **96**

Herb and Pistachio Dressing (gf) (v) **212**

Herby Yoghurt Mayo (gf) (v) **212**

Hot and Sweet Dipping Sauce (gf) (v) **94**

Japanese-style Dressing (v) **16**

Lemon, Tarragon and Mustard Mayo (gf) (v) **213**

Lemony Yoghurt Dressing (gf) (v) **118**

Lime and Jalapeño Mayo (gf) (v) **80**

Mignonette Dressing (gf) (v) **16**

Miso and Sesame Mayo (v) **214**

Miso and Spring Onion Butter (v) **86**

Olive Salsa (gf) (v) **74**

Parmesan, Walnut and Garlic Mayo (gf) (v) **124**

Peanut Dressing **122**

Pico de Gallo (gf) (v) **92**

Pineapple Sambal **214**

Pistachio Salsa (gf) (v) **146**

Russian Dressing (gf) (v) **30**

Salsa Verde Mayo (gf) **216**

Salted Caramel Sauce (gf) **216**

Satay Sauce (v) **217**

Smoked Paprika Mayo (gf) (v) **12**

Smoky Chilli Butter (gf) (v) **78**

Smoky Paprika and Sherry Vinegar Mayo (gf) (v) **218**

Soy and Lime Dipping Sauce (v) **217**

Tahini Yoghurt (gf) (v) **128**

| | |
|---|---|
| Tarragon Aioli (gf) (v) | 130 |
| Tartare Sauce (gf) (v) | 218 |
| Tomato, Capsicum and Chilli Relish | 219 |
| White Barbecue Sauce | 88 |

**COOKIES**

| | |
|---|---|
| Chunky Toblerone and Roasted Macadamia Cookies | 196 |
| Double Chocolate, Roasted Peanut and Tahini Skillet Cookie (gf) | 174 |
| Passionfruit Shortbread | 206 |

**CORN**

| | |
|---|---|
| Grilled Corn with Whipped Ricotta and Smoky Chilli Butter (gf) (v) | 78 |

**COUSCOUS**

| | |
|---|---|
| Eggplant, Spinach and Couscous Salad with Lemony Yoghurt Dressing (v) | 118 |
| *Crayfish with Miso and Spring Onion Butter* | 86 |
| *Crisp Lettuce and Asparagus Salad with Tarragon Aioli and Soft Eggs (gf)* | 130 |
| *Crispy Chicken and Bacon Burgers* | 142 |
| *Crispy Spiced Onion Fritter Burgers with Mango Chutney (v)* | 140 |
| *Curried Mango Chutney Mayo (gf) (v)* | 211 |

# D

| | |
|---|---|
| *Double Chocolate, Roasted Peanut and Tahini Skillet Cookie (gf)* | 174 |

**DRINKS**

| | |
|---|---|
| Chilled Espresso Martini Affogato (gf) | 156 |
| Christmas Champagne Cocktail | 32 |
| Elderflower G&T | 34 |
| Gibson Martini | 34 |
| Horse's Neck | 32 |
| Michelada | 26 |
| Morning Start-up | 32 |
| Negroni | 34 |

# E

**EGGPLANT**

| | |
|---|---|
| Eggplant, Spinach and Couscous Salad with Lemony Yoghurt Dressing (v) | 118 |
| Luscious Tomatoes, Baked Eggplant and Mozzarella Salad (gf) (v) | 120 |
| *Eggplant, Spinach and Couscous Salad with Lemony Yoghurt Dressing (v)* | 118 |

**EGGS**

| | |
|---|---|
| Crisp Lettuce and Asparagus Salad with Tarragon Aioli and Soft Eggs (gf) | 130 |
| Two-bean and Crisp Flatbread Salad with Soft Eggs (v) | 106 |

*Elderflower G&T*    34

**ESPRESSO**

Chilled Espresso Martini Affogato (gf)    156

Tiramisu Espresso Martini No-bake Cheesecake    178

# F

**FENNEL**

Fresh Fennel, Salami and Chilli Pizza    48

**FETA**

Baked Prawns with Lemon and Feta (gf)    56

Lemony Sumac Chicken and Chickpea Salad with Dates, Feta and Baby Spinach    110

**FISH**

Best-ever Fresh Catch Beer-battered Fish    60

Fish Tacos with Pico de Gallo    92

Market Fish with Green Olive, Jalapeño and Tomato Salsa (gf)    54

Mexican Fish Tacos with Avocado and Jalapeño Sauce    24

*Fish Tacos with Pico de Gallo*    92

*Fresh Fennel, Salami and Chilli Pizza*    48

**FRITTERS**

Crispy Spiced Onion Fritter Burgers with Mango Chutney (v)    140

Prawn, Zucchini and Lemongrass Fritters (gf)    18

# G

*Gibson Martini*    34

**GINGER**

Sticky Fingers Ginger Loaf with Butterscotch Glaze    190

**GOAT'S CHEESE**

Avocado, Broad Bean and Goat's Cheese Salad (gf) (v)    132

*Greens, Ricotta and Mushroom Pizza (v)*    46

*Grilled Corn with Whipped Ricotta and Smoky Chilli Butter (gf) (v)*    78

*Grilled Steak Sandwich with Caramelised Onions and Mushrooms*    84

*Grilled Zucchini with Tzatziki and Kasundi (gf) (v)*    70

# H

**HALOUMI**

Haloumi and Peach Kebabs (gf) (v)    76

Moroccan Lamb Burgers, Grilled Haloumi and Pistachio Salsa    146

*Haloumi and Peach Kebabs (gf) (v)*    76

*Herb and Pistachio Dressing (gf) (v)* **212**

*Herby Yoghurt Mayo (gf) (v)* **212**

*Honey-roasted Apricots (gf)* **213**

*Horse's Neck* **32**

# I

**ICE CREAM**

Chilled Espresso Martini Affogato (gf) **156**

Lemon Meringue and Blueberry Pie Ice Cream **162**

Luscious Baklava and Pistachio Ice Cream **154**

Rockmelon and Gin Slushies (gf) **160**

Summer Fruits in a Lemongrass and Citrus Syrup (gf) **166**

# K

**KEBABS**

Haloumi and Peach Kebabs (gf) (v) **76**

Lamb and Bacon-wrapped Date Kebabs (gf) **76**

Prawn and Chorizo Kebabs with Smoked Paprika Mayo (gf) **12**

*Kiwi Lamb Burgers* **138**

*Knock-your-socks-off Croutons, Fresh Tomato, Prosciutto and Mozzarella Salad* **108**

# L

**LAMB**

Barbecued Butterflied Leg of Lamb with Herb and Parmesan Dressing (gf) **96**

Kiwi Lamb Burgers **138**

Lamb and Bacon-wrapped Date Kebabs (gf) **76**

Moroccan Lamb Burgers, Grilled Haloumi and Pistachio Salsa **146**

*Lamb and Bacon-wrapped Date Kebabs (gf)* **76**

*Late Summer Crumble* **180**

**LEMON**

Baked Prawns with Lemon and Feta (gf) **56**

Classic Lemon Tart **172**

Lemon Meringue and Blueberry Pie Ice Cream **162**

Lemon, Tarragon and Mustard Mayo (gf) (v) **213**

*Lemon Meringue and Blueberry Pie Ice Cream* **162**

*Lemon, Tarragon and Mustard Mayo (gf) (v)* **213**

*Lemongrass and Garlic Roasted Pork Belly* **64**

| | |
|---|---|
| *Lemony Sumac Chicken and Chickpea Salad with Dates, Feta and Baby Spinach* | **110** |
| *Luscious Baklava and Pistachio Ice Cream* | **154** |
| *Luscious Tomatoes, Baked Eggplant and Mozzarella Salad (gf) (v)* | **120** |

# M

| | |
|---|---|
| *Macadamia Caramel Tart* | **176** |

**MACADAMIAS**

| | |
|---|---|
| Chunky Toblerone and Roasted Macadamia Cookies | **196** |
| Macadamia Caramel Tart | **176** |

**MANGO**

| | |
|---|---|
| Barbecued Pork, Mango and Herb Salad | **112** |
| Smoked Chicken and Mango Salad with Crispy Noodles and Peanut Dressing | **122** |
| Summer Fruits in a Lemongrass and Citrus Syrup (gf) | **166** |
| *Market Fish with Green Olive, Jalapeño and Tomato Salsa (gf)* | **54** |
| *Mexican Fish Tacos with Avocado and Jalapeño Sauce* | **24** |
| *Michelada* | **26** |
| *Miso and Sesame Mayo (gf) (v)* | **214** |
| *Mixed Tomato Salad with Tahini Yoghurt and Crisp Capers (gf) (v)* | **128** |
| *Morning Start-up* | **32** |
| *Moroccan Lamb Burgers, Grilled Haloumi and Pistachio Salsa* | **146** |

**MOZZARELLA**

| | |
|---|---|
| Knock-your-socks-off Croutons, Fresh Tomato, Prosciutto and Mozzarella Salad | **108** |
| Luscious Tomatoes, Baked Eggplant and Mozzarella Salad (gf) (v) | **120** |
| Prawns with Nectarines, Mozzarella and Prosciutto (gf) | **20** |
| Spicy Salami, Prosciutto and Mozzarella Pizza | **44** |

**MUFFINS**

| | |
|---|---|
| Ramp Them Up Blueberry Streusel Muffins | **186** |
| *Mushroom Arancini (v)* | **28** |
| *Mushroom and Caramelised Onion Pizza (v)* | **42** |

**MUSHROOMS**

| | |
|---|---|
| Greens, Ricotta and Mushroom Pizza (v) | **46** |
| Grilled Steak Sandwich with Caramelised Onions and Mushrooms | **84** |
| Mushroom Arancini (v) | **28** |
| Mushroom and Caramelised Onion Pizza (v) | **42** |

## N

*Negroni* — 34

**NECTARINES – SEE STONE FRUIT**

**NOODLES**

Roasted Veg and Udon Noodle Salad (v) — 114

## O

*Oaty Muesli Slice* — 202

*Olive Oil and Orange Cake with Honey-roasted Apricots* — 158

*One-pot Chocolate Cake with Sour Cream and Chocolate Frosting* — 194

**ONIONS**

Beer and Hoisin-braised Onions (v) — 210

Caramelised Onions (gf) (v) — 211

Chicken with Yoghurt, Caramelised Onions and Cashew Nuts (gf) — 98

Crispy Spiced Onion Fritter Burgers with Mango Chutney (v) — 140

Grilled Steak Sandwich with Caramelised Onions and Mushrooms — 84

Mushroom and Caramelised Onion Pizza (v) — 42

**ORANGES**

Olive Oil and Orange Cake with Honey-roasted Apricots — 158

*Oysters on the Half Shell* — 16

## P

*Passionfruit Shortbread* — 206

**PASTA**

Baked Tomatoes and Spaghetti (v) — 50

Chilli Prawn Pasta — 52

**PEACHES – SEE STONE FRUIT**

**PEANUTS**

Double Chocolate, Roasted Peanut and Tahini Skillet Cookie (gf) — 174

Satay Sauce (v) — 217

*Pineapple Sambal* — 214

**PISTACHIOS**

Herb and Pistachio Dressing (gf) (v) — 212

Luscious Baklava and Pistachio Ice Cream — 154

Moroccan Lamb Burgers, Grilled Haloumi and Pistachio Salsa — 146

Roasted Beetroot, Blue Cheese and Pistachio Salad (gf) (v) — 126

**PIZZA**

Cacio e Pepe Pizza (v) — 40

Fresh Fennel, Salami and Chilli Pizza — 48

Greens, Ricotta and Mushroom Pizza (v) — 46

| | |
|---|---|
| Mushroom and Caramelised Onion Pizza (v) | 42 |
| Pizza Dough (v) | 215 |
| Spicy Salami, Prosciutto and Mozzarella Pizza | 44 |
| *Pizza Dough (v)* | *215* |

**PLUMS – SEE STONE FRUIT**

**PORK**

| | |
|---|---|
| Barbecued Pork, Mango and Herb Salad | 112 |
| Lemongrass and Garlic Roasted Pork Belly | 64 |
| Sticky Tamarind and Maple Syrup Glazed Pork Ribs | 72 |

**POTATOES**

| | |
|---|---|
| Chips (gf) (v) | 60 |
| Warm Roasted Potato Salad with Parmesan, Walnut and Garlic Mayo (gf) (v) | 124 |
| *Prawn and Chorizo Kebabs with Smoked Paprika Mayo (gf)* | *12* |
| *Prawn, Zucchini and Lemongrass Fritters (gf)* | *18* |

**PRAWNS**

| | |
|---|---|
| Baked Prawns with Lemon and Feta (gf) | 56 |
| Chilli Prawn Pasta | 52 |
| Chipotle Prawns with Lime and Jalapeño Mayo (gf) | 80 |
| Chorizo and Garlic Prawn Burgers | 144 |
| Prawn and Chorizo Kebabs with Smoked Paprika Mayo (gf) | 12 |
| Prawn, Zucchini and Lemongrass Fritters (gf) | 18 |
| Prawns with Nectarines, Mozzarella and Prosciutto (gf) | 20 |
| *Prawns with Nectarines, Mozzarella and Prosciutto (gf)* | *20* |

**PROSCIUTTO**

| | |
|---|---|
| Knock-your-socks-off Croutons, Fresh Tomato, Prosciutto and Mozzarella Salad | 108 |
| Prawns with Nectarines, Mozzarella and Prosciutto (gf) | 20 |
| Spicy Salami, Prosciutto and Mozzarella Pizza | 44 |

**PUMPKIN**

| | |
|---|---|
| Spiced Pumpkin Cheesecake Tart | 170 |

# R

| | |
|---|---|
| *Ramp Them Up Blueberry Streusel Muffins* | *186* |
| *Reuben Sliders* | *30* |
| *Rhubarb and Strawberry Frangipane Tarts* | *168* |

**RIBS**

| | |
|---|---|
| Beef Short Ribs | 90 |

Sticky Tamarind and Maple Syrup
Glazed Pork Ribs **72**

**RICE**

Baked Spanish Rice with Chicken
and Chorizo (gf) **62**

Mushroom Arancini (v) **28**

**RICOTTA**

Greens, Ricotta and Mushroom
Pizza (v) **46**

Grilled Corn with Whipped Ricotta
and Smoky Chilli Butter (gf) (v) **78**

*Roast Salmon with Pomegranate
Glaze and Herby Yoghurt Mayo (gf)* **58**

*Roasted Beetroot, Blue Cheese
and Pistachio Salad (gf) (v)* **126**

*Roasted Veg and Udon Noodle
Salad (v)* **114**

*Rockmelon and Gin Slushies (gf)* **160**

# S

**SALADS**

Avocado, Broad Bean and Goat's
Cheese Salad (gf) (v) **132**

Barbecued Pork, Mango and
Herb Salad **112**

Crisp Lettuce and Asparagus Salad with
Tarragon Aioli and Soft Eggs (gf) **130**

Eggplant, Spinach and Couscous Salad
with Lemony Yoghurt Dressing (v) **118**

Knock-your-socks-off Croutons,
Fresh Tomato, Prosciutto and
Mozzarella Salad **108**

Lemony Sumac Chicken and
Chickpea Salad with Dates, Feta
and Baby Spinach **110**

Luscious Tomatoes, Baked Eggplant
and Mozzarella Salad (gf) (v) **120**

Mixed Tomato Salad with Tahini
Yoghurt and Crisp Capers (gf) (v) **128**

Prawns with Nectarines, Mozzarella
and Prosciutto (gf) **20**

Roasted Beetroot, Blue Cheese
and Pistachio Salad (gf) (v) **126**

Roasted Veg and Udon Noodle
Salad (v) **114**

Seeded Slaw (gf) (v) **104**

Smoked Chicken and Mango Salad with
Crispy Noodles and Peanut Dressing **122**

Spice-roasted Carrot and Avocado
Salad (gf) (v) **116**

Two-bean and Crisp Flatbread Salad
with Soft Eggs (v) **106**

Warm Roasted Potato Salad with
Parmesan, Walnut and Garlic
Mayo (gf) (v) **124**

**SALAMI**

Fresh Fennel, Salami and Chilli Pizza **48**

Spicy Salami, Prosciutto and
Mozzarella Pizza **44**

**SALSA – SEE CONDIMENTS**

*Salsa Verde Mayo (gf)* — 216

**SALMON**

Roast Salmon with Pomegranate Glaze and Herby Yoghurt Mayo (gf) — 58

*Salt and Pepper Squid* — 22

*Salted Caramel Sauce (gf)* — 216

**SANDWICHES AND SLIDERS**

Chicken Katsu Sliders — 14

Grilled Steak Sandwich with Caramelised Onions and Mushrooms — 84

Reuben Sliders — 30

*Satay Sauce (v)* — 217

**SAUCES – SEE CONDIMENTS**

*Sausage Coil with Charred Broccolini and Avocado and Olive Salsa (gf)* — 74

**SEAFOOD – SEE CRAYFISH, FISH, OYSTERS, PRAWNS AND SQUID**

*Seeded Slaw (gf) (v)* — 104

**SLICES**

Coconutty Fudge Slice — 200

Oaty Muesli Slice — 202

Take Me With You Cherry, Almond and Coconut Slice — 188

*Smoked Chicken and Mango Salad with Crispy Noodles and Peanut Dressing* — 122

*Smoky Paprika and Sherry Vinegar Mayo (gf) (v)* — 218

*Soy and Lime Dipping Sauce (v)* — 217

*Spice-roasted Carrot and Avocado Salad (gf) (v)* — 116

Spiced Pumpkin Cheesecake Tart — 170

*Spicy Salami, Prosciutto and Mozzarella Pizza* — 44

**SQUID**

Salt and Pepper Squid — 22

*Steak Tacos with Charred Pineapple Salsa* — 82

*Sticky Fingers Ginger Loaf with Butterscotch Glaze* — 190

*Sticky Tamarind and Maple Syrup Glazed Pork Ribs* — 72

**STONE FRUIT**

Boozy Barbecued Stone Fruit Parcels — 164

Haloumi and Peach Kebabs (gf) (v) — 76

Late Summer Crumble — 180

Olive Oil and Orange Cake with Honey-roasted Apricots — 158

Summer Fruits in a Lemongrass and Citrus Syrup (gf) — 166

**STRAWBERRIES – SEE BERRIES**

*Summer Fruits in a Lemongrass and Citrus Syrup (gf)* — 166

# T

**TACOS**

| | |
|---|---|
| Fish Tacos with Pico de Gallo | 92 |
| Mexican Fish Tacos with Avocado and Jalapeño Sauce | 24 |
| Steak Tacos with Charred Pineapple Salsa | 82 |
| *Take Me With You Cherry, Almond and Coconut Slice* | *188* |
| *Tartare Sauce (gf) (v)* | *218* |

**TARTS**

| | |
|---|---|
| Classic Lemon Tart | 172 |
| Macadamia Caramel Tart | 176 |
| Rhubarb and Strawberry Frangipane Tarts | 168 |
| Spiced Pumpkin Cheesecake Tart | 170 |
| *Tiramisu Espresso Martini No-bake Cheesecake* | *178* |
| *Tomato, Capsicum and Chilli Relish* | *219* |

**TOMATOES**

| | |
|---|---|
| Baked Tomatoes and Spaghetti (v) | 50 |
| Knock-your-socks-off Croutons, Fresh Tomato, Prosciutto and Mozzarella Salad | 108 |
| Luscious Tomatoes, Baked Eggplant and Mozzarella Salad (gf) (v) | 120 |
| Mixed Tomato Salad with Tahini Yoghurt and Crisp Capers (gf) (v) | 128 |
| Tomato, Capsicum and Chilli Relish | 219 |
| *Two-bean and Crisp Flatbread Salad with Soft Eggs (v)* | *106* |

# W

| | |
|---|---|
| Walnut Praline (gf) | 220 |
| Warm Roasted Potato Salad with Parmesan, Walnut and Garlic Mayo (gf) (v) | 124 |
| Whipped Avocado with Silken Tofu, Lime and Jalapeño (gf) (v) | 10 |
| A Wicked Chocolate and Apricot Loaf (gf) | 192 |

# Y

**YOGHURT**

| | |
|---|---|
| Chicken with Yoghurt, Caramelised Onions and Cashew Nuts (gf) | 98 |
| Coconut Yoghurt Loaf | 198 |
| Herby Yoghurt Mayo (gf) (v) | 212 |

# Z

**ZUCCHINI**

| | |
|---|---|
| Grilled Zucchini with Tzatziki and Kasundi (gf) (v) | 70 |
| Prawn, Zucchini and Lemongrass Fritters (gf) | 18 |

dish.co.nz | DISH 237

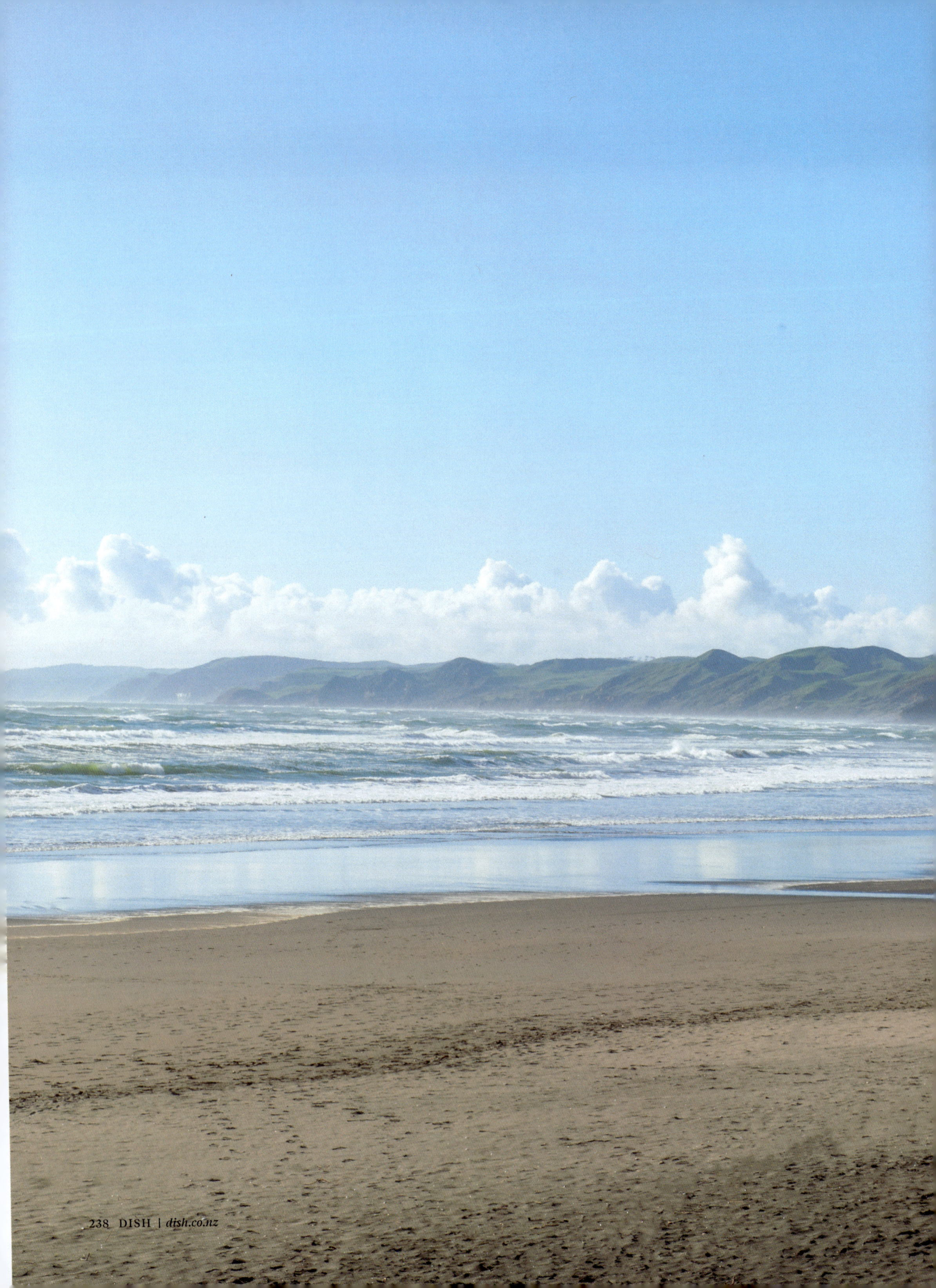

# Acknowledgements

*dish* magazine is New Zealand's favourite foodie title for good reason – consistently delivering achievable, simple recipes that are always in tune with the season. *dish SUMMER* brings together a compilation of our favourite warm-weather recipes from the last few years. Authors *dish* editor and stylist Sarah Tuck and *dish* food editor Claire Aldous are delighted to bring these recipes together into one easy, take-anywhere cookbook.

Sarah Tuck is fiercely passionate about creating recipes that are simple to make, taste delicious and look spectacular on the plate (occasionally also getting behind the camera to take a few shots), while Claire Aldous brings her wealth of knowledge and expertise to share with gusto and selfless dedication.

Long-time *dish* contributor, the brilliantly talented photographer Josh Griggs, is always an absolute delight to work with. His skill and impeccable eye combined with unparalleled technical skill result in images that shine. He also comes with a side order of sass and some bloody good Spotify playlists.

Not one, not two, but three amazing SCG designers have been on the tools wrangling the words and pictures into the stunning book you now hold in your hands. Huge thanks to Conor Fox, Chrisanne Terblanche and Archie Blohm – you guys rock!

Sanguine, multi-talented *dish* deputy editor Maddie Ballard has triple-checked the recipes and taken on the mammoth task of index creation with nary a qualm, while joint SCG managing directors Fred Soar and David Atkins and CEO Marcus Hawkins-Adams have fulsomely encouraged the team in their extra-curricular publishing project.

To all the above, a heart-felt thank you... and I can't wait to see what we get up to next!

Published by SCG Media
www.scg.net.nz
Printed by SCG
20 Vestey Drive, Mt Wellington, Auckland 1060, New Zealand

Copyright © SCG Media 2022
Design copyright ©SCG Media 2022
Photography copyright © Josh Griggs 2022
Except photographs on page 4 © Ben Whorwood,
page 7 © Carolyn Haslett, page 38 and 39 © Olivia Galletly,
pages 23, 25, 27, 68, 69, 79, 81, 83, 134, 135, 150, 151, 152, 153, 182,
183, 184, 185, 207, 237, 238 © Sarah Tuck
Editor and stylist: Sarah Tuck
Recipes: Claire Aldous and Sarah Tuck
Photography: Josh Griggs and Sarah Tuck
Art direction and design: Conor Fox, Chrisanne Terblanche
and Archie Blohm
Copy editor: Maddie Ballard

All rights reserved. Without limiting the rights under copyright reserved above, no part of this publication may be reproduced, stored in or introduced into a retrieval system, or transmitted in any form or by any means (electronic, mechanical or photocopying, recording or otherwise), without the prior written consent of both the copyright owners and the publisher of this book.

Printed and bound in New Zealand by SCG

ISBN 978-0-473-63486-5

dish.co.nz
Facebook: Dishmagazine
Instagram: dishmagnz

Printed in Great Britain
by Amazon